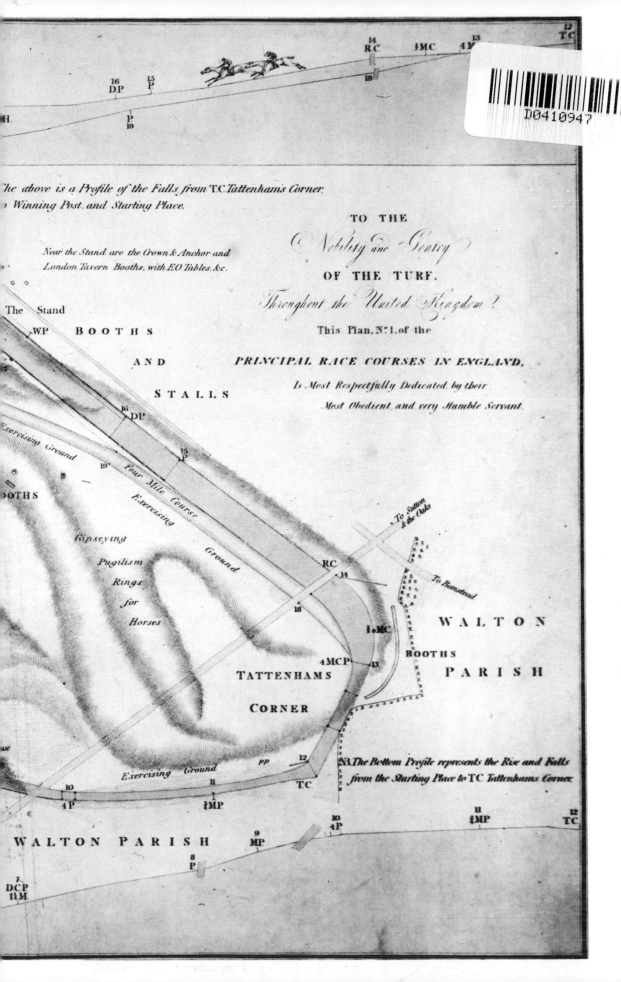

The Official Story of
The Blue Riband of the Turf

DERBY
200

Michael Seth-Smith
Roger Mortimer

Guinness Superlatives Limited
2 Cecil Court, London Road, Enfield, Middlesex

Acknowledgements

The authors and publishers wish to record their gratitude for particular help given by:

Arthur Ackermann & Son Ltd.

James Bishop, Esq, *Illustrated London News*.

Mrs Mark Dessain, *The British Racehorse*.

Charles Fornara, Esq, Berkeley Hotel, London.

Hodder and Stoughton Limited for permission to publish extract on page 54 from *My Story* by Sir Gordon Richards.

Charles J L Langlands, Esq.

Stephen Ling, Esq, Fores Gallery, London.

Peter J. Matthews, Guinness Superlatives Ltd.

Marcus Marsh, Esq.

Pelham Books for permission to publish extracts on pages 72–75 from *Racing with the Gods* by Marcus Marsh.

The Stewards of the Jockey Club, Newmarket.

The Trustees of the British Museum.

United Racecourses Ltd.

signifies the official approval of United Racecourses Ltd. and the Jockey Club.

Editor: Beatrice Frei

Illustrative Research: Beatrice Frei, Tim Neligan and Beverley Waites

Index: Anna Pavord

Published in Great Britain by Guinness Superlatives Ltd, 2 Cecil Court, London Road, Enfield, Middlesex

Set in 10/11 Times Roman

Colour separation by Newsele Litho Ltd, London and Milan

Printed and bound by Jarrold & Sons Ltd, Norwich

ISBN 0 900424 79 6

Contents

Foreword

The Rt Hon Earl of Derby, MC, DL

𝔎𝔫𝔬𝔴𝔰𝔩𝔢𝔶

Almost everything to do with the naming of the Derby is surmise and one can only suppose that the success of the Oaks, first run in 1779, and the fact that my ancestor, the 12th Earl of Derby, had won the race, inspired him to think of greater things. He was a very popular man, a good landlord and a fine gentleman, but his way of life was extremely lackadaisical. He lived for the day and cared nothing for the future or the past.

However, it does seem fairly clear that the Derby was conceived at a dinner party at 'The Oaks' at which Sir Charles Bunbury was present. Some doubt is thrown on the story that he and Sir Charles tossed up to decide whether the race should be called the 'Derby' or the 'Bunbury'. My grandfather always maintained that the story was true.

Certainly the first few runnings of the Derby attracted little attention, so it is in many ways surprising that the race was to grow into one of such international influence. The two hundredth running of the Derby is creating worldwide interest—I believe that this excellent book captures the essence of its importance both to horse racing and as a part of Britain's heritage.

Edward Stanley, 12th Earl of Derby (1752–1834) by Thomas Gainsborough
(the Earl of Derby, MC)

SECTION 1

The origins of the Derby

The origins of the Derby are interwoven with the careers of two men, John Burgoyne who was renowned as a swashbuckling gambler, playwright, wit and soldier, and Edward Smith Stanley, his nephew by marriage. Without their close association the Epsom Derby, famous as the greatest horse race in the world, might never have been established.

Edward's father, James Smith Stanley, who designated himself 'Lord Strange' even though he had no legal right to the title, was the eldest son of the 11th Earl of Derby and had been educated at Westminster School; his best friend there was John Burgoyne, reputedly an illegitimate son of Lord Bingley. The two boys, of whom Burgoyne was the junior by some 4 years, shared a passionate interest in the theatre and spent much of their leisure hours writing and acting their own plays. After leaving Westminster in 1735 James Stanley went to Leyden University and completed the Grand Tour. Burgoyne became a cornet in the 13th Light Dragoons and 5 years later purchased a lieutenancy in the

regiment which was stationed at Preston, less than 20 miles from the Derby ancestral home, Knowsley. Due to his friendship with James Stanley, Burgoyne was shown considerable hospitality at Knowsley, but the hospitality ceased abruptly when it was discovered that the penniless soldier had eloped with James's sister, Lady Charlotte Stanley. Family fury erupted and the young couple were banished to London where they lived in virtual poverty before mounting debts compelled them to flee to France. As an exile Burgoyne learned to speak French fluently, and travelled extensively throughout Europe, making a particular study of French, German and Italian military systems. In 1756 he returned to England, rejoined the army, and rapidly gained a reputation as an efficient and enterprising officer who was also a dandy, and possibly no more than an unscrupulous and ambitious adventurer.

Meanwhile, in March 1747, James Stanley had married Lucy, daughter and co-heiress of Hugh Smith of Weald Hall, Essex who provided a dowry of £100 000 for his daughter. Their first son, christened Edward, was born in September 1752, 2 years before 'Lord Strange' was elected to the Jockey Club. As the years went by 'Lord Strange' found pleasure in introducing his son to the sports and pastimes in which he was interested. Thus the boy grew up finding enjoyment in all outdoor sports, including the Turf, especially when his father took him to the Isle of Man where he raced many of his own horses and ponies; and he had a race named 'the Derby' in his honour. 'Lord Strange' was a Member of Parliament for Lancashire, and after 'Gentleman Johnny' Burgoyne—by 1763 a Colonel with a gallant war record and with his misdemeanours forgiven by the Stanley family—was elected as Member for the Midhurst division of Sussex, the two men renewed their close friendship. Inevitably the stories of battles, wars and bravery under enemy fire excitingly recounted and perhaps exaggerating the part played by the hero, appealed to young Edward Stanley who was enthralled by the stories of Burgoyne's exploits and achievements— achievements enhanced when his prestige and income were increased as a result of his appointment as commandant of Fort William in Scotland.

Burgoyne's new affluence enabled him to purchase an old inn near Epsom which had been part of a property owned by the Lambert family for 500 years and more recently was used as the headquarters of a group of local hunters and sportsmen. Burgoyne considered Epsom ideal for his new home for it was less than 20 miles from London and racemeetings had been held on the Downs for more than a century. During the Civil War a party of Royalists had met there 'under pretext of a horse-race, intending to cause a diversion on the King's behalf' and after the fall of the Commonwealth further race-meetings were organised with King Charles II attending one of them. From 1730 onwards racemeetings were held annually with the usual custom of the day's sport commencing at 11 am and after two or three heats had been run, the racing fraternity adjourning to Epsom and the surrounding villages for lunch and refreshment before racing was resumed in the afternoon. In more recent years constant victories by the locally trained champion, Eclipse, had brought further fame to an area of Surrey whose renown as the centre of the healthgiving 'Epsom salts' was steadily declining.

Burgoyne enlarged his Epsom home, built on a dining-room, added stabling and outbuildings, and gave the estate the name 'The Oaks' since massive oak trees grew in the vicinity of the house. Diarist and socialite Charles Greville described the house, which Burgoyne boasted could accommodate 50 guests for the local race-meeting, as 'a very agreeable place, with an odd sort of house, built in different times, and by different people, but the outside is covered with ivy and creepers which is very pretty . . .'.

Soon local villagers gleaned reports of night-long parties held at The Oaks and of reckless gambling by Burgoyne's guests who included Charles James Fox, Richard Brinsley Sheridan, 'Lord Strange' and his 16-year-old son Edward.

In June 1771 Lord Strange died suddenly at the age of 54 and young Edward, an undergraduate of Trinity College, Oxford, found himself spending more and more time accepting the guidance and the hospitality of Burgoyne. When he announced his engagement to Lady Elizabeth Hamilton, only daughter of the 6th Duke of Hamilton, Burgoyne organised a lavish, extravagant and expensive fête-champêtre at The Oaks in honour of the engaged couple. Especially for the occasion he wrote a masque The Maid of the Oaks which was performed in a pavilion designed by Robert Adam. The evening cost the staggering sum of £5000, with the garden transformed by the importation of hundreds of orange trees and other exotic plants in addition to imitation haycocks made of yellow velvet adorned with rows of fairy-lights. Edward Stanley was immensely grateful to Burgoyne who became tantamount to his 'father confessor'; and as the soldier encouraged his nephew's sporting inclinations, particularly the ownership of racehorses and the making of substantial wagers, it seemed that Edward was becoming increasingly self-indulgent and profligate. Although now elected as a Member of Parliament for Lancashire, he had countless parasitic hangers-on and gave the impression that he was prepared to enjoy a dissolute existence. He began making matches with his horses against those of Sir Charles Bunbury, the Duke of Grafton, Lord Foley and Sir John Lade, but refused to tolerate Colonel O'Kelly who lived with his mistress, the notorious Charlotte Hayes, at Clay Hill near Epsom where he entertained some of the nobility and all of the lowest dregs of blacklegs* and prize-fighters.

In 1775, the year after Edward Stanley's marriage, 53-year-old Burgoyne was one of the three British Generals sent to America in an effort to subdue the 'turbulent colonists'. Although vain, Burgoyne was sufficient of a realist to appreciate the rewards and honours which a grateful nation would bestow upon him if he could return from the New World as a conquering hero. Before he sailed across the Atlantic he leased The Oaks to Edward Stanley —the transaction suiting both men admirably.

While Burgoyne was in America the 11th Earl of Derby died and Edward Stanley succeeded his grandfather becoming 12th Earl of Derby and

* In the 18th and early 19th century this was the common term for bookmakers.

Left: Sir Charles Bunbury (1740 1821), the most influential member of the Jockey Club during the final decade of the 18th century. Engraving by John Watson after a painting by Sir Joshua Reynolds. (Trustees of the British Museum) *Right:* The 3rd Duke of Grafton (1735–1811), by Batoni. Prime Minister of England and successful owner-breeder of Thoroughbreds, who won three Derbies with Tyrant (1802), Pope (1809) and Whalebone (1810). (National Portrait Gallery, London)

inheriting vast estates in Lancashire. Lady Charlotte Burgoyne's finances also improved, for she received £25 000 and an annuity of £400 under her father's will. Sadly she died months later, leaving her newly inherited wealth to her adventurous husband who within 2 years had ignominiously surrendered to the Americans at Saratoga before returning to England with his reputation at its lowest ebb. Charles James Fox referred to him as 'a gallant officer sent like a victim to be slaughtered where his own stock of personal bravery would have earned him laurels if he had not been under the hands of blunderers'. But despite Fox's plea he remained in the wilderness for 4 years, a lonely widower who turned for solace to the 12th Earl of Derby who was viciously described as 'a nobleman who started his political career on the true, genuine principles of aristocracy . . . his ancestors were generally men of distinguished merit. The present Peer degenerates from their virtues and if not infamous, his deportment renders him contemptible . . .' The unhappy Burgoyne and the 12th Earl of Derby spent more and more time in each other's company, particularly at Knowsley and The Oaks,

with the General advising his nephew upon his bloodstock interests. He also elaborated upon the success of his military acquaintance Anthony St Leger who had inaugurated a new race for three-year-olds at Doncaster in the autumn of 1776.

They decided to organise a similar contest for fillies over the last 1½ miles of the Epsom course, giving the race the title of 'the Oaks' as a compliment to Lord Derby who usually acted as a steward of the Epsom meetings. To the delight of the majority the race was won in 1779 by Lord Derby's Bridget who defeated her eleven rivals including fillies owned by Lord Egremont, Sir Charles Bunbury and the unpopular O'Kelly.

The success of Bridget was celebrated by the winning owner in sumptuous fashion at a dinner that he gave at The Oaks that evening, 14 May. One of his guests was Bunbury, his senior by some twelve years, and also educated at Westminster. Bunbury, embittered by the lengthy legal proceedings of his petition for divorce from the lovely Lady Sarah Lennox and the ensuing publicity, was turning his whole-hearted attention to the Turf, concentrating particularly upon his stud at Barton Hall, his home

near Bury St Edmunds. Although only 38 years of age he was the most active member of the Jockey Club and acknowledged as its undisputed leader. He held strong views upon every aspect of racing, seldom bet but made it abundantly clear that he raced his horses only for profit. In an age renowned for brutality he never allowed his jockeys or his stable-lads to touch his horses with a whip and was unwilling for them to wear spurs, believing that such ill-treatment made their mounts restive and vicious. A contemporary wrote:

> Whatever might be the faults and peccadillos of Sir Charles Bunbury, he was a man naturally benign, of compassionate and friendly disposition, and his plan for treating racehorses, without suffering them to be abused by the whip and spur which he laboured so long and steadfastly, though unsuccessfully, to make general on the Turf, ought ever to be remembered in his honour.

He was vehemently opposed to the customary sweating gallops, and made every effort to discourage the excessive 4- and 6-mile races which he was convinced were distressing and detrimental for the thoroughbred.

Other guests at The Oaks on the night of Bridget's triumph included Burgoyne, Fox and Sheridan. During the evening it was proposed and resolved that the following year a race for three-year-old colts should be organised and contested. Conditions were drawn up and eventually it was pointed out that the race should have a name. As the name would honour one of the subscribers and sponsors or one of their horses, it was only natural that the titles 'Bunbury', 'Burgoyne' and 'Derby' were bandied about in the discussion, although no mention was made of 'The O'Kelly' or 'The Eclipse'. John Burgoyne would dearly have loved to have had his own name immortalised, but to no avail. Eventually, and possibly on the toss of a coin or the turn of a card, the title 'the Derby' was agreed upon to the evident pleasure of the host. Thus the world's greatest horse-race originated.

At the time that the first Derby was contested, Lord North, a man whose incompetence was continually overlooked by King George III, was Prime Minister. Ten years earlier Captain Cook had discovered New South Wales, and in the intervening decade Warren Hastings had been appointed first Governor-General of India, oxygen had been discovered by Joseph Priestley, and Doctor Samuel Johnson had retained his pre-eminence as the literary lion of London although he had celebrated his 70th birthday. In truth the inaugural Derby was of little importance except to the subscribers and the locals who were present on 4 May 1780 when Sir Charles Bunbury's Diomed* defeated his eight opponents. The race, which started in the parish of Banstead half a mile east of Tattenham Corner, was run over a straight mile. Many of the 'curled and scented bucks, with their cambrics and quizzing glasses and sparkling rings' who attended the day's sport had danced at a ball the previous night and showed little interest in the proceedings from fatigue and boredom. They and their ladies of quality arrived on the Downs in their cabriolets, post-chaises and carriages, and were stared at by the villagers who were unaccustomed to such luxury. No one present had any conception of the historic importance of the occasion, and the Derby was considered no more than an incidental contest which was included in the afternoon's sporting programme to decide which of the subscribers' thoroughbreds was the best three-year-old miler. These subscribers included the Duke of Cumberland who gave the patronage of the Royal family to the race from its inception. There were no preliminary heats, and the newly instituted idea of having one race to decide the winner was not acceptable to some reactionaries. The Derby was judged by Mr Hilton, the Jockey Club judge at Newmarket, who had been persuaded to travel to Epsom to act in his official capacity, and it was arranged that Mr Samuel Betts, the Jockey Club starter, should also assist in the proceedings.

The following year O'Kelly's Young Eclipse won the Derby, much to the disgust and chagrin of the Jockey Club who steadfastly refused to contemplate electing him to their exclusive Club. Yet the record of his horses in the Derby prior to his death in 1787 was remarkable. In his colours of 'scarlet, black cap' Budrow was second to Diomed (1780), Young Eclipse won (1781), Dungannon was second (1783), Sergeant won (1784) and Gunpowder was second (1787) to Sir Peter Teazle owned by Lord Derby. This colt owed his name to the fact that the 12th Earl of Derby had become infatuated with the actress Elizabeth Farren whom he had first seen when she was playing the leading role in the London production of *The Heiress*, a successful play that had been written by Burgoyne while he was living with his mistress at Knowsley. Elizabeth Farren was the daughter of a County Cork surgeon and apothecary, and when she played Lady Teazle in

---

* Diomed and other particularly noteworthy Derby winners mentioned in the following pages are documented in greater detail in section 3 by Roger Mortimer.

John Burgoyne (1722–92)—Soldier, gambler and playwright—who married Lady Charlotte Stanley and subsequently influenced his nephew by marriage, the future 12th Earl of Derby. A portrait by Allan Ramsay painted in Rome. (National Portrait Gallery, London)

Sheridan's *School for Scandal* he named a filly 'Lady Teazle' and a colt 'Sir Peter Teazle' in her honour. Eventually, after the death of his wife in 1797, Lord Derby married her. By the time of his death in 1834 the Derby was renowned as the greatest and most important horse-race in the world.

The year after Sir Peter Teazle won the Derby for the 12th Earl of Derby, victory was achieved by Sir Thomas, the first odds-on favourite to succeed, and a colt owned by the Prince of Wales, who drove from Carlton House to Epsom in a carriage drawn by four horses with postilions and preceded by outriders. Leaving London at 8 am the royal party arrived at the racecourse shortly before the first race was contested, and took up their position in The Prince's stand which had been especially constructed for the royal guest, and which appeared from the exterior to be a small, flat-topped edifice with battlements in the style of a mid-European castle. The town of Epsom was packed to capacity, with accommodation almost impossible to procure, and one gentleman who wished to hire a house for race-week was asked for the equivalent of 2 years' rent. However, the victory of Sir Thomas was immensely popular and encouraged the Prince of Wales to believe that his destiny was to be found upon the Turf.

During the last decade of the 18th century the Derby remained of little significance, and even its most ardent supporters gave priority to discussing the French Revolution and the appalling news of atrocities in Paris. There was no newspaper coverage of the race, the power of the Jockey Club was not yet absolute in administering race-meetings, and officials found it difficult to control the crowds, estimated at 5000, who came to the Downs for the afternoon's entertainment. Transport facilities for spectators were minimal, and the thoroughbreds who contested the race had to be walked from their training quarters to Epsom. The journey from Newmarket took weeks and consequently fields were small and for the most part made up of locally trained horses. For the first four years the Derby was run over a distance of a mile, and only in 1784 was this distance increased to 12 furlongs, with the start taking place on the south side of the Downs and obscured from the view of those standing by the winning-post.

In 1801 Sir Charles Bunbury again won the Derby when Eleanor triumphed, thus becoming the first filly to succeed. The following day she trounced her opponents in the Oaks, but her trainer, Cox, saw neither of her victories. Hours before the Derby he was taken ill, but reputedly with his dying breath gasped to the astonished parson by his side. 'Depend upon it, Eleanor is a hell of a mare.'

For the next 15 years, for most of which time England was in the midst of her titanic struggle against Napoleon Bonaparte, the Derby continued to play but an inconsequential part on the racing scene. In 1803 the Earl of Derby's Sir Peter Teazle had the distinction of siring the first three placed by the judge, and between 1802 and 1815 Lord Egremont owned the Derby winner on three occasions and the 3rd Duke of Grafton on four occasions. The Duke, a great-grandson of King Charles II, became Prime Minister in 1766 and remained in office for 4 years despite scandalising society and the nation by publicly flaunting his mistress. However, he deserves high praise for improving the breed of thoroughbred by the mating of his mares at his famous Euston Hall Stud with the 1793 Derby winner Waxy. One of his colts, Tyrant, who won the 1802 Derby was described by Nimrod as 'one of the worst horses ever to have won the Derby'; but the Duke was again successful when Pope won in his 'sky blue' colours in 1809 and gained a third victory the subsequent year with Whalebone who, like Blucher and Whisker, was sired by Waxy. The Duke's greatest rival on the Turf was Lord Egremont who won the Derby five times between 1782 and 1826 but he may have had more than his share of good fortune for his trainer, Bird, confessed on his deathbed that at least two of his master's Derby winners were four-year-olds. However, he had the grace to add that neither Lord Egremont nor the jockey were parties to the deception.

In 1821 Gustavus became the first grey to win the Derby. He was sired by Lord Egremont's Derby-winner Election, and ridden by Sam Day, member of the famous racing family who lived at Stockbridge. It was a hot, sunny afternoon and a great number of spectators had not waited until 1.30 pm, when the Derby was due to be run, before invading the refreshment tents and booths. They consumed beer and spirits freely and liberally and in consequence little notice was taken of the attempts by the groundsmen and officials who were paid 18 pence a day, to clear the course. After the race Sam Day complained 'Buckle and I wound in and out all the way from Tattenham Corner like a dog at a Fair'. Frank Buckle, who rode five Derby winners, was the most famous jockey of the era and had been born in 1766 at Newmarket, where his father was a saddler. He thought nothing of riding on his hack from his home in Peterborough to Newmarket, a distance of almost 50 miles, to ride exercise gallops, and return home in time for late tea. The status of professional jockeys was low, but Buckle did much to enhance it and for almost half a century rode with the coolest of judgement and the strongest of nerve. Towards the end of Buckle's career he was rivalled by Jem Robinson who was born at Newmarket in

1794 and was considered by the locals 'to have taken to riding like the very devil' while still in his teens. In 1824 he achieved a remarkable wager, having bet that within 7 days he would ride the winner of the Derby, the winner of the Oaks and get married. In total he rode six Derby winners: Azor (1817), Cedric (1824), Middleton (1825,), Mameluke (1827), Cadland (1828), and Bay Middleton (1836).

Before the end of the 1820s the Epsom racecourse became the focal point of intrigue which eventually resulted in the founding of the Epsom Grandstand Association. Charles Bluck, a north-country character of dubious origin approached John Briscoe, Member of Parliament and Lord of the Manor, and proposed that he should build on the Downs a grandstand for the accommodation of visitors to the races. Persuasive in his approach he explained the great success of the new grandstand built at Doncaster and emphasised his proposal by implying that the Jockey Club were entirely agreeable to the scheme and fully supported it. Briscoe, either gullible or disinterested, accepted the proposal without first checking the credentials of Bluck, and on 28 November 1828 a lease was signed giving Bluck an acre of land for 90 years at £30 per annum. In return he promised to build a brick or stone grandstand within a year and to spend at least £5000 on its construction. News of Bluck's intentions spurred others, appalled at the artful speculation of the northerner, to establish an association with Sir Robert Wilson, the Hon Robert King, Sir James Alexander and C N Palmer Esq the first Trustees for building a grandstand which would accommodate 5000 people and would contain suitable refreshment rooms, offices and other apartments. Pressure was brought to bear upon Bluck to part with his lease for £750, and the contract made with Mr Chadwick to build the grandstand was transferred to the new lessees. In truth Bluck had stolen a march on those who had the future of the Derby at heart, and financially had to be 'bought off'. Had he refused to be coerced into parting with his lease from Briscoe, albeit at considerable profit, the future of the Derby could have been in jeopardy.

In January 1829 the foundations of the grandstand, 150 ft in width and 60 ft in depth, with a magnificent flight of steps in the centre, were laid. The cost was £14 000, the money being raised by an issue of 100 £20 shares, with a further £5000 being raised by a mortgage on the property which was designed by William Trendall. Although he was instructed by the newly formed Epsom Grandstand Association, whose first committee meeting was held at the King's Head, Poultry, to omit all unnecessary ornamentation in the grandstand in order to decrease extra costs, the grandstand had two major defects. There was very little seating accommodation except on the open top of the stand which had no roof, and as the stand was built parallel to the course few spectators had an unobstructed view of the races. Financially the grandstand also had difficulties once built, one of them being the fact that the wretched Bluck insisted on being granted an under-lease for four rooms on the ground floor which he used to serve refreshments. Thus some of the profit went to him instead of the Association. Another set-back was the fact that the approach made to members of the Royal family for patronage was declined, so that the new grandstand did not receive the hoped-for accolade. In addition, the actual construction fell behind schedule and at one time it was thought the grandstand would not be completed in time for the 1830 Derby. However, despite all teething troubles it was duly announced on Monday, 12 April 1830 on the front page of the *Morning Chronicle*.

EPSOM GRAND STAND

The Committee beg to inform the Nobility and Gentry frequenting Epsom Races, that this elegant building will be ready for the reception of company at the ensuing Meeting, which commences on the 25th May. The Committee have provided a room for the Members of the Jockey Club and the New Rooms at Newmarket, and for the Stewards of the Races. The remainder of the building, comprising a convenient betting-room, saloon, balcony, roof, refreshment, and separate retiring-room for Ladies, with attendance and other accommodations, WILL be OPEN to the PUBLIC. Refreshments of every description will be provided by Mr Charles Wright at the most reasonable prices, a list of which will be seen at the Stand. The whole arrangement will be under the direction of the Committee, who are resolved that the strictest order shall be preserved. Ladies and Gentlemen will find their pleasure and comfort greatly increased by repairing to the Stand, as they will enjoy a full view of the whole Course. They will have the Grand Saloon, which is 110 feet by 40, as a promenade, and they will have every accommodation around them. The advantages of which, when compared with the confinement of a carriage, are obvious. Prices of admission, Tuesday and Wednesday, 3s each: Thursday and Friday, 5s each. Tickets for the week 12s.

The Magistrates for the county of Surrey are respectfully informed that they will be admitted free.

7 Oxendon-street, *April 7*.

(Significantly, the address in Oxendon-street, was the headquarters of Weatherbys.)

By 1830 the Derby had been established for 50 years—but the complexion of racing had changed. No longer were thoroughbreds owned exclusively by the aristocracy and the nobility, and the new class of owners, many of them of unsavoury

Above: Sir Peter Teazle (Highflyer—Papillon), who won the 1787 Derby; bred by Lord Derby at Knowsley. Painting: English School, 19th century. (The Earl of Derby, MC)

Left: Frank Buckle (1766–1832), the outstanding jockey of the era, who rode five Derby winners between 1792 and 1823. Painting attributed to Harry Hall. (The Jockey Club, Newmarket)

character, was doing nothing to alleviate the disrepute into which the Turf was remorselessly sinking. Bookmakers and unscrupulous rogues of the calibre of Crockford, Gully and Ridsdale were sinister characters prepared to stop at nothing to achieve their designs. Horses were nobbled, jockeys bribed and gamblers ruined by such men who employed the lowest of scoundrels to carry out their nefarious plots. Matters came to such a pitch that Greville felt compelled to write in his *Diary*:

> The sport of horseracing has a peculiar and irresistible charm for persons of unblemished probity. What a pity it is that it makes just as strong appeal to the riff-raff of every town and city.

The gaming-houses of London, and the racecourses became the haunts of these men and those of timid nature were made unwelcome on the courses which were inefficiently run and organised. There were no

Bay Middleton (Sultan—Cobweb), the third and final Derby winner owned by the 5th Earl of Jersey; by James Pollard. The colt had a vicious temper and a doubtful leg, and after his 1836 Derby triumph was bought by Lord George Bentinck. (Arthur Ackermann & Son Ltd)

'A Start for the Derby, or the Effects of a Windy Day'—A view on the Epsom Course 1820. (Fuller's Sporting Gallery, 1820. Courtesy NS Collin, Esq)

Priam (Emilius—Cressida), winner of the 1830 Derby and originally bought by Newmarket trainer William Chifney for one thousand guineas as an unbroken yearling. (The Parker Gallery)

number-boards giving details of the runners, no organised parades or appearances in the paddock before the race, and little punctuality in the times of the races. Yet villainy and skulduggery were gradually to disappear and be replaced by new standards of honesty and efficiency in early Victorian England. The advent of railways heralded a new era in transport which rapidly aided the conveyance of people and goods despite the outcry of a Member of the House of Commons:

Was the House aware of the smoke and the noise, the hiss and the whirl which locomotive engines, passing at the rate of ten or even twelve miles an hour, would occasion? . . . it would be the greatest nuisance, the most complete disturbance of quiet and comfort in all parts of the kingdom that the ingenuity of man could invent.

The conditions of entry for the Derby and the prize-money at stake inevitably caused the race to take pre-eminence, and by 1830 the value to a winner had risen to £2800—a huge sum by the standards of the day. The popularity of the race and the enormous crowds who thronged the Downs had resulted in county magistrates being admitted free and a room in the grandstand put at their disposal for the retention of prisoners. In 1829 a policeman attended the Derby in his official capacity for the first time and the Association was presented with a bill for £7 for his services and those of his helpers.

Priam who won the 1830 Derby was one of the greatest horses ever to triumph at Epsom, and few would dispute the assertion that he was the best horse to achieve victory in the first 50 years of the Derby's history. Sired by 1823 Derby winner Emilius out of Cressida, sister to Derby and Oaks

heroine Eleanor, Priam was bred by Sir John Shelley who had already owned two Derby winners Phantom and Cedric. Referring to Priam, John Kent the Goodwood trainer subsequently wrote:

I have seen all the best horses that have flourished and had their day for more than sixty years past, and I now repeat my well-considered opinion that Priam was the most perfect racehorse that I have ever seen. His constitution was magnificently sound; his temperament and nervous system beautifully attuned; his shape, make and action were faultless. No weight known to the Racing Calendar could crush his spirit. All courses came alike to him.

Priam, trained at Newmarket by W. Chifney, had been bought as a yearling for 1000 gns and did not run as a two-year-old. He won two races at Newmarket in the spring of 1830 before leaving for Epsom on a journey graphically described by Turf historian 'The Druid':

With four companions Priam left Newmarket at four o'clock in the morning of the Friday the week before the Derby. Will Chifney and his pony caught them up before they had completed the twenty-one miles to Newport. On the second day Will put some of the commissariat across his pony's back and walked the remainder of the journey by the side of his favourite. All along the road Priam was an object of interest. His fame had been noised abroad, and the way-side innkeepers were on the look-out for the 'Newmarket nag'. On the Saturday night a halt was made at 'The Cock' at Epping and the following morning long before church was over, the procession had passed down Piccadilly and reached stables at the top of Sloane Street. The next day the walk was resumed and in due course Priam reached Mickleham Downs and so had nine clear days in which to complete his preparation for the Derby.

The Chifneys made a fortune when Priam won the Derby, and they became the spoilt darlings of society. Yet it caused their downfall ultimately, for they suffered, like so many others, from vaulting ambition. In 1834 they believed that Shillelagh was a certainty for the Derby and backed him accordingly. His defeat by Plenipotentiary caused them to return to Newmarket dispirited and virtually ruined.

In 1836 Jem Robinson, who had ridden his first Derby winner 19 years previously, won on Lord Jersey's Bay Middleton. The afternoon was marred for many of the nobility when it was learned that 60-year-old Hon Berkeley Craven had shot himself at his home in Connaught Terrace as a consequence of not being able to settle his betting losses on the race. This tragedy so upset the young Captain Rous who had attended the Derby with his bride that he became a confirmed antagonist of gambling for the remainder of his life.

Two years later when the Derby was won by Amato, owned by Sir Gilbert Heathcote who lived at The Durdans which adjoined the racecourse, the London and South Western Railway Company ran special excursion trains on their Southampton line from their Nine Elms terminal. There was no station near Epsom where passengers could alight, but it was arranged that eight trains would stop at a point where the railway crossed the Kingston to Ewell road, some 5 miles from the racecourse. The railway officials were flabbergasted at the number of racegoers who arrived at the Nine Elms depot early on the morning of Derby Day, and the eight trains were totally inadequate to accommodate all those who clamoured for tickets. Such a demand was an indication of the popularity of the Derby with Londoners, many of whom drove the 17 miles to Epsom, each and every year. The roads would be choked with traffic, and horses who usually pulled a small load around the streets of the East End would be required to travel the best part of 40 miles in one day. Not surprisingly there were countless breakdowns of both horses and their carts which suffered broken wheels and axles on the uneven roads. Every tavern along the route would be jam-packed with racegoers. Some of whom never arrived at the racecourse. Rogues, pick-pockets and thieves had a field-day and cab-drivers made a fortune from their exorbitant charges. Amato never ran again after his 1838 Derby victory, and eventually was buried at The Durdans. One of the local inns had its name altered to 'The Amato' and a legend was nurtured that at dawn on each Derby Day the name of the winner would be chalked up on the side of a well outside the inn.

Dorling's genuine card list—Derby Day 1827. (Photograph from *Epsom and the Dorlings* by E E Dorling, published by Stanley Paul)

'The Winner', by James Pollard, 1842. (Arthur Ackermann & Son Ltd)

Ever since the formation of the Epsom Grand-stand Association the driving force had been William Dorling. The Dorlings were originally a Suffolk family, but William who had a small but flourishing printing and stationery business at Bexhill, decided to seek pastures new and moved to Epsom which in the early 19th century was still no more than a pleasant village, with some 350 houses and a population of less than 3000. In his Epsom shop William Dorling sold writing-paper, hymn-books, lavender-water and cakes of shaving-soap, and rapidly became a respected and influential citizen. Always enterprising and an opportunist he saw the advantages of going on to the Downs on the mornings of the race-meetings, collecting every scrap of information from the trainers and grooms concerning the afternoon's runners and then rushing post-haste back to his printing-press to produce Dorling's '*Only Genuine Racecard Approved by Authority*' which bore the signatures of the Right Hon the Earl of Derby, John Maberly Esq, MP and J. Farrall, clerk of the course; he hawked and sold these later in the day to spectators at the race-meeting. He had no competitors and quickly established a monopoly, although his offer in 1830 to mention the prices of admission to the new grandstand at the bottom of his racecard and to state that the horses would be saddled in front of the stand was not accepted by the Committee. However, it was implied that any future printing regarding the races needed by the Committee would be given to him, for he had astutely taken up shares when the Epsom Grandstand Association was formed. A decade later Dorling had consolidated his position to such an extent that he was able to arrange for his son Henry to become the clerk of the course, and it was he who was responsible for the festive arrangements made to greet the young Queen Victoria when she came to Epsom to see the 1840 Derby. The Committee were thrilled that at long last royalty was once again to patronise the Derby and spared neither effort nor expense to ensure that the occasion was a success. The paddock was turned into a ground for the royal promenade and the saddling, watched by the Prince Consort, took place in Langley Bottom. The race was won by Little Wonder, the smallest horse ever to win the Derby, for he only measured a mere 14 hands 3½ in

Yet all had the common denominator of sharing a day which was part of their nation's heritage, and within minutes of the Derby being run, carrier pigeons were dispatched to every major city giving details of the result.

Bentinck's second justification for Derby immortality concerns the 1848 winner Surplice, whose dam Crucifix was a daughter of the mighty champion Priam, and who had been bred by Bentinck. Yet when Surplice triumphed at Epsom he did not do so in the 'sky blue, white cap' of Bentinck for he had impulsively sold his racing empire to Mr Mostyn at Goodwood in 1846. The day after the Derby Disraeli met a disconsolate Bentinck in the House of Commons Library. Disraeli who had recently been honoured with the Garter and was very concious of the prestige of the blue Garter sash that he was entitled to wear, tried to soothe the misery of Bentinck who told him: 'All my life I have been trying for this, and for what have I sacrificed it. You do not know what the Derby is.' 'Yes I do', replied Disraeli, 'it is the Blue Riband of the Turf.'

Throughout the next two decades Henry Dorling consolidated his position and that of the Epsom Grandstand Association. A man of many talents, he was exceedingly musical—and able to play five wind instruments—and had immense personal charm. As his second wife he married Elizabeth Jerram, whose daughter Isabella Mary, born in 1836, by her first husband Benjamin Mayson, was to attain world fame as the authoress of a cookery book after her marriage to Mr Beeton. She and her two sisters lived for many years in the grandstand at Epsom, but were evacuated during the Derby meeting to Brighton where Henry Dorling was also clerk of the course. Dorling once complained to his wife that being a clerk of the course was not a gentleman's job. To which she replied, 'You are a gentleman, Henry, so you have made it so.' As a small boy Henry had attended a school in Bexhill for the sons of German legionaires stationed there during the Napoleonic Wars, and throughout his life began the Lord's Prayer 'Unser Vater . . .'. In 1850 the Association accounts showed a small initial profit, and he considered that the time had come to procure more land both for building and course improvement. Grandiose schemes were put forward to increase the size of the grandstand and include a weighing-room and offices for the stewards, the clerk of the course and the clerk of the scales, but the scheme did not come to fruition. However, although the prestige of the racecourse was becoming enhanced, Dorling was finding his own position untenable due to his financial obligations. In 1865 he made it abundantly clear that he had no desire to renew his 21-year lease which was about to

Lord George Bentinck (1802–48), by S. Lane. His energy and investigation disclosed the 'Running Rein' fraud. He was described by Disraeli as 'Lord Paramount of the Turf'. (National Portrait Gallery, London)

expire. As an alternative he offered to manage the grandstand for the Association, and at a shareholders' meeting he and the Chairman, Francis Knowles Esq, were appointed Joint Managing Directors at salaries of £500 a year.

Meanwhile the middle of the 19th century found several champions among the Derby winners. In 1853 West Australian became the first Triple Crown winner, while four years later Blink Bonny repeated the triumphs of Eleanor by winning both the Derby and the Oaks. With any luck on her side Blink Bonny might have won four Classics during the season. She was never nominated for the Two Thousand Guineas, was unplaced in the One Thousand Guineas when not fully recovered from dental trouble which had plagued her all the previous year, and was deliberately pulled by her villainous jockey who had been bribed by an equally villainous bookmaker in the St Leger. Second to Blink Bonny in the Derby was Black Tommy, a 200–1 outsider owned by Mr Drinkald who took a bet of £10 000 to a suit of clothes about the chance of his colt. Until the judge announced that Blink Bonny had won by a neck the bookmaker who

'Derby Day', by WP Frith. (After the original in The Tate Gallery. Photo courtesy The Parker Gallery)

accepted the bet was in a state of apoplexy. Within seven years Blink Bonny had added greater glory to her reputation by becoming the dam of Blair Athol who had never seen a racecourse before his Derby victory. The pride of England's leading bloodstock-

breeders, basking in the reflected glory of Blair Athol's triumph, and pontificating over the assured success of breeding a Derby winner from a Derby winner, received a very rude shock the year after Blair Athol's victory, for Gladiateur, owned by a

The grandstand on Derby Day, 1846. (*Illustrated London News*)

Derby jockeys in the weighing-room, 1846. (*Illustrated London News*)

Frenchman and sired by a French stallion, not only won the Triple Crown but also the Grand Prix de Paris.

In the final 30 years of the 19th century the Derby was won by some of the greatest heroes in its history, including Galopin, Bend Or, Iroquois,

Ormonde, Isinglass, Persimmon and Flying Fox. These and other champions were owned by the new aristocracy whose wealth had become prodigious due both to the enormous increase in land values, particularly in London, and to the immense prosperity in the world of banking and commerce. The era was also halcyon owing to the high standard of riding exemplified by Fred Archer and George Fordham, and the brilliant training achievements of John Porter and Matthew Dawson. Above all else, however, it was the era of the Prince of Wales and his Marlborough House set.

Epsom suffered a severe loss in 1873 with the death of Henry Dorling who, for more than half a century, had been associated with the racecourse as clerk of the course; lessee of the grandstand, general manager of the Association, and printer of the official racecards. In the final years of his life he had been involved in protracted negotiations as the lessors, including the owners of Walton Manor, demanded higher rents. The year before his death the present Derby course was used for the first time. The start was slightly further from the grandstand and on higher ground, thus lessening the steep ascent in the first 3 furlongs. Henry Mayson Dorling who succeeded his father as clerk of the course was determined to make the racecourse and the grandstand as complete and independent as possible. He acquired land north, west and east of the grandstand and built a new east wing to the

Lord Falmouth and Fred Archer (1857–86). His achievements, including five Derby victories, captured the imagination of the general public to a greater extent than any other jockey. (The Jockey Club, Newmarket)

Epsom Downs on a Derby morning. (*Illustrated London News*)

stand, while in 1879 he was able to lease 5 acres at Tattenham Corner which allowed a straight 5-furlong course to be layed out. A decade later he was responsible for the Association buying Walton Downs, an extent of 205 acres including Tattenham Corner and the training grounds known as 'Six Mile Hill'. Not content with this advantageous purchase he subsequently obtained a 29-year lease of Epsom Downs which included leases of all the buildings on the Downs other than those already the property of the Association, thus strengthening still further the influence of the Association upon the race-meetings held at Epsom in general and the Derby in particular.

An anticipated feature of every Derby Day during this era was the presence of the elderly Sir John Bennett, clockmaker and jeweller of Cheapside, who would ride his cob amongst the crowd between the grandstands and Tattenham Corner. His eccentricity was widely known, and he would stop every few yards to drink 'the health of the people' with anyone who offered him a glass of ale. A fine figure of a man with a flowing white beard and ruddy countenance, he was affectionately referred to as 'jolly Sir John' and was an institution

without which no Derby Day was complete.

In 1870 the Derby was won by Kingcraft, owned and bred by Lord Falmouth. One of the most respected of Victorians he never bet, and during the 13 years from 1870 to 1883 he had the good fortune to win 14 Classics. Throughout this period when Matthew Dawson was training the horses bred at his Mereworth Stud, his jockey was Fred Archer who had been apprenticed to Dawson who described him as 'that damned long-legged, tin scraping young devil'. Archer had his first ride in the Derby in 1874 when he was unplaced on King of Tyne. The next year he finished third on Lord Falmouth's unnamed colt by Macaroni, having already ridden both the Two Thousand Guineas and One Thousand Guineas winners, and being about to ride the Oaks winner two days later. He was again unplaced in the Derby in 1876 riding Skylark for his patron, but at his fourth attempt in 1877 won on Silvio, wearing Lord Falmouth's famous 'black, white sleeves, red cap'. At the time of this triumph Archer was 20 years of age, taller than most of his contemporaries, conservative in his dress and his demeanour, and totally dedicated to the task of riding winners. So strong was this

Piccadilly Circus on the morning of Derby Day, 1864. (*Illustrated London News*)

dedication that on one occasion he was found in tears, miserable that he could not ride both winners in a dead-heat His father had ridden the 1858 Grand National winner, and as a boy he was riding ponies almost as soon as he could walk. Blessed with nerves of iron and an uncanny judgement of pace he was an opportunist with the ability to sum up the chances not only of his own mount but of his rivals while a race was in progress. Never the most elegant of jockeys he invariably conjured up the strongest of finishes although he preferred to ride with a slacker and looser rein than his contemporaries. He had two faults—both caused by his burning ambition for victory. The first was that he could be excessively harsh upon the horses that he rode, and the second the tactical lengths to which he would go to defeat his opponents. There was no draw for positions at the start and Archer believed that he was entitled to the most favourable, almost by divine right. Woe betide anyone who attempted to foil him. He excelled at Epsom, especially on the big occasion and seemed the supreme master of the undulating track. His greatest rival was George Fordham who was 20 years his senior and who only once was victorious in the Derby, winning on Sir

Bevys in 1879. Fordham's riding was graphically described:

> He rode with fairly short leathers, got well down on his mount's back, and slewed his head and body almost sideways during a race with his shoulders hunched up high.

Sir Bevys was a very moderate colt, owned by Baron Lionel de Rothschild who at the time raced under the name of 'Mr Acton'. The race was run on sodden and very heavy going, and Fordham wisely elected to race almost under the grandstand rails once the straight was reached, and where the ground was less saturated. His tactics succeeded, and although his victory was acclaimed due to his popularity, few backed the winner except the Poet Laureate, Lord Tennyson, who took £100–£5 'because Sir Bevys was the hero of one of my early poems'.

Archer's second Derby victory came in 1880 when he won on the 1st Duke of Westminster's Bend Or (Doncaster–Rouge Rose) trained by Robert Peck at Russley Park near Swindon. The life of the 1st Duke of Westminster spanned the entire Victorian era, for he was born in 1825, the year that

'The Derby Day'—eight chromo-lithographs by Hablot K. Browne (Phiz), *c*. 1863.

The Epsom Carnival (*Illustrated London News*)

Left: Epsom 1881—Iroquois (F. Archer) the Derby hero, and beneath Bend Or and Robert the Devil who fought an epic duel in the Cup (*Illustrated London News*)

Below: Derby heroes of 1879–1888—1 Bend Or, 2 Harvester, 3 Melton, 4 St Gatien, 5 Sir Bevys, 6 Ormonde, 7 Iroquois, 8 Shotover, 9 Merry Hampton, 10 Ayrshire, 11 St Blaise. (*Illustrated London News*)

the Stockton–Darlington Railway was opened and died in 1899, the year that the Boer War began and gold was found on the Klondyke. Popular with men in all walks of life it was claimed that 'The Duke could pass from a race meeting to a missionary meeting without incurring the censure of even the strictest . . . his name is a household word throughout the land.' The Duke's interest in racing was fostered by his eldest son and by Lord Rosebery who proposed that Peck should become their private trainer.

In 1875 Peck persuaded the Duke to buy the five-year-old Doncaster for £14 000. Two years previously Doncaster had won the Derby and only a fortnight before the sale to the Duke he had won the Ascot Gold Cup. In retrospect it could be claimed that the Duke of Westminster's Turf success was mere luck for as 'The Special Commissioner' wrote:

> Had not Doncaster been more or less thrust upon him by Robert Peck after the horse had been more or less refused by the old Cobham Stud Co., it is questionable whether the Duke would ever have figured at all on the Turf to any appreciable extent . . . .

Fourth in Doncaster's Derby was Chandos, who three years later was to start a very short-priced favourite for the Grand National.

A month before he was due to ride Bend Or in the Derby Archer was severely shaken and his arm muscles badly torn when he was savaged by a four-year-old on Newmarket Heath. Only the brave action of fellow jockey, J. Goater, who with whip flourishing and yelling at the top of his voice, rode straight at the maddened horse saved Archer from death. As it was, Archer was unable to ride for more than a week, his weight rose alarmingly to over 10 st, and a Harley Street specialist fitted him with an iron contraption which he wore to apply pressure to his arm muscles. Determined to be physically fit to give of his brilliant best to Bend Or he was stunned to learn on the eve of the race that Bend Or had developed sore shins and might not run. However, the 'invalids' triumphed in one of the most exciting Derby finishes ever witnessed, with Bend Or defeating Robert The Devil by a head. To prove how great a champion the runner-up was, he won the Grand Prix de Paris within a month of his Derby defeat. Two furlongs from home in the Derby Robert The Devil was clear, with the race seemingly at his mercy. However, Archer, refusing to admit defeat, continued to urge Bend Or foward with almost superhuman strength. As he did so Robert The Devil's jockey, Rossiter, made the unpardonable mistake of looking round and causing his mount momentarily to become unbalanced. As Bend Or closed on him, Robert The Devil rallied, and the two champions matched strides as the winning-post

approached. Yards from the finish they were level, but at the line Archer had forced the Duke's colt into the lead, the judge awarding the distances as a head and a bad third.

The Duke, who also ran Muncaster in the Derby and had declined to make a declaration favouring either colt, went to the telegraph office in the grandstand immediately after leading in his hero and sent a telegram to his son who was an undergraduate at Christ Church, Oxford. The curt telegram read 'Bend Or first'. There was no signature and no comment upon the glorious victory. Only an immensely affluent man could have favoured such brevity upon such an occasion.

A fortnight after the Derby there was a dramatic sequel which resulted in a *cause célèbre* when the owner of Robert The Devil approached the senior steward of the Jockey Club and informed him that he intended to object to the winner on the grounds that Bend Or was not the colt that he was purported to be. He claimed that in reality the dam of the Derby winner was Clemence and not Rouge Rose, and that the two colts of whom Clemence and Rouge Rose were the dams had been confused when they were sent from the Eaton Stud to Russley Park to be put into training. After a lengthy hearing at which the principal witness for the plaintiff was an Eaton stud groom the objection was overruled, although in the course of the evidence it became apparent that the Eaton Stud was administered on haphazard lines. The Duke of Westminster always believed that Bend Or was correctly described and did not hesitate to send Clemence to Bend Or. Significantly, her first foal was 'of weak intellect to say the least, who has to be accompanied by a white ass wherever she goes . . .'.

For the remainder of the season the epic Derby struggle between Bend Or and Robert The Devil was discussed *ad infinitum*, with the adherents and supporters of the two great horses vehemently praising the merits of their favourite. Bend Or won the St James's Palace Stakes at Royal Ascot, but in the autumn there could be little doubt that 'The Devil' was the better, for he trounced Bend Or in both the St Leger and the Champion Stakes in addition to winning the Cesarewitch carrying 8 st 6. He must be considered one of the greatest horses *not* to have won the Derby. Bend Or beat him a head in the 1881 Coronation Cup at Epsom and proved an infinitely more successful stallion when retired to stud.

The day before the memorable Coronation Cup victory of Bend Or, Iroquois won the Derby, ridden by Archer who hugged the inside position so closely as the runners rounded Tattenham Corner that his boot was ripped from toe to heel. It was a historic occasion for Iroquois was bred at the Erdenheim

Lord Rosebery's Ladas, by Emil Adam. (The Jockey Club, Newmarket)

Stud near Philadelphia. When the news of his triumph reached New York, business on Wall Street was temporarily suspended, and the Stock Exchange was the scene of gigantic celebration. Among those who finished unplaced behind Iroquois in the Derby was Lord Rosebery's Voluptuary who years later won the Grand National at Aintree. His achievements did not end with this success for subsequently he was bought by an actor and for many months during the long run of *The Prodigal Daughter* at Drury Lane Theatre he came on to the stage at every performance and jumped a miniature water-jump. There was no doubt that Iroquois was an exceptionally good colt who went on to win the St Leger, yet he was not the best American-bred three-year-old in England during the season, for the record of Foxhall, sired by Lexington who was a direct descendant of Diomed, was outstanding. Never entered for the English Classics Foxhall won the Grand Prix de Paris, the Cesarewitch and the Cambridgeshire before further enhancing his reputation by victory

in the 1882 Ascot Gold Cup.

The year 1884 saw the first dead-heat for the Derby, between St Gatien and Harvester, and the following year another brilliant victory for Fred Archer who rode Melton to a head victory over Paradox after one of the closest struggles ever witnessed throughout the final furlong. The huge crowds at Epsom realised that Archer was nothing if not a genius in the saddle, and gave him a stupendous reception as he rode back to the hallowed winner's enclosure. After the race Lord Hastings, owner of Melton, received a telegram from Oscar Wilde: 'I understand that Milton's "Paradise Lost" is being revived and will appear in Derby Week and will be published under the title "Paradox Lost" by Melton.' For F. Webb who rode Paradox the defeat was especially unwelcome, for it was the fifth consecutive Derby in which he had been placed without a victory.

'The Tinman' was now lionised from Land's End to John O'Groats and to endorse his mastery of Epsom won the Derby again the next year when he

The filming of the 1895 Derby by Bert Acres. (Science Museum)

rode the Duke of Westminster's Ormonde to a convincing victory. Ormonde, sired by Bend Or in his first season at stud, went on to capture the Triple Crown. So great was the public admiration for Ormonde that it was seriously suggested that the Duke, who was Master of The Horse, should ride his hero in the 1887 Jubilee Procession. John Porter who trained Ormonde advocated the proposal and assured the Duke that Ormonde would 'go as quiet as a sheep'. Ultimately the idea was discarded and instead a garden party given in honour of Ormonde at Grosvenor House, the Duke's Park Lane mansion. Early on the morning of the reception the mighty horse left Kingsclere, was unboxed at Waterloo and walked across Westminster Bridge and through St James's Park. Among the guests who fêted him were the Prince and Princess of Wales, the Prince and Princess William of Prussia, and the Kings of Belgium and Denmark.

It was becoming fashionable for foreign royalty and aristocrats to attend the Derby, but the Epsom Grandstand Association decided to take no action

in 1892 when they received a telegram from the Grand Duke Alexis who was on a visit to England: 'Kindly postpone Derby until 4 pm. Have missed train. Grand Duke Alexis.'

Another Triple Crown winner emerged in 1893 when Mr H. McCalmont's Isinglass triumphed in all three Classics. Runner-up to Isinglass in the Derby was Ravensbury, ridden by H. Barker who three months earlier had been second in the Grand National on Aesop. It was a popular success, as was that of Ladas 12 months later, for Ladas was owned by Lord Rosebery who at the time of the Derby was Prime Minister. Thirty years earlier Lord Palmerston, while Prime Minister, had owned a Derby runner, Maidstone, but the colt had finished unplaced to Thormanby. Within hours of returning from Epsom to London jubilant at his success, Lord Rosebery received a telegram from a well-wisher, 'Only heaven now left.' The victory was also hailed as a local success at Epsom, for Lord Rosebery had bought The Durdans estate from the Heathcote family. His wife Hannah Rothschild was the daughter of Baron Mayer Rothschild who had built the vast mansion of Mentmore where the thoroughbreds who raced in the primrose and rose hoops were bred. As if 1894 was not sufficient of an *annus mirabilis* for Lord Rosebery he won the Derby again in 1895 with Sir Visto, a horse not considered in the same class as Ladas. Yet Sir Visto's Derby success was memorable in that it was the first occasion upon which 'moving pictures' of the Derby were taken. Pioneer photographer Birt Acres mounted his kinetic camera on a massive tripod in a small wooden stand by the winning-post and took pictures of the horses racing up the straight from Tattenham Corner. These pictures and those taken earlier in the afternoon by Acres including shots of the police clearing the course and the preliminary canter of the Derby contestants are historic.

The victories of Ladas and Sir Visto were overshadowed by the happiest Derby result in 1896 when the winner was owned by Albert Edward, Prince of Wales. The Prince, 55 years of age, had shown interest in the Turf for almost two decades, but had enjoyed little success and in the past eight seasons had only won £6000 in stakes. In 1890 he had written to his friend Henry Chaplin whose colt Hermit had won the 1867 Derby. In the course of the letter the Prince commented that, although he could never expect to have the good fortune which attended the Dukes of Portland and Westminster, he still hoped that with patience he might win one or more of the Classics with a horse that he had bred. His visits to Epsom, Ascot and Newmarket were popular with the crowds who attended the meetings and although at times, particularly during the Tranby Croft affair, he was criticised in certain sections of the Press, there was little doubt that sporting England longed above all else for the Prince to own a Derby winner.

The colt who achieved this glorious result was Persimmon, sired by St Simon out of Perdita II a mare bought for the Prince by John Porter. At the end of the 1892 season the Prince had moved his horses from Kingsclere to Newmarket to be trained by Richard Marsh, ostensibly so that he could drive from Sandringham to see them at exercise, but more likely because his racing manager, Lord Marcus Beresford, and Porter did not see 'eye to eye'. Marsh had recently built Egerton House, the most palatial and modern training establishment in the kingdom, on land leased from Lord Ellesmere. To finance the huge expense Lord Ellesmere put aside a sum of £50 000, this being the surplus earned by his stallion Hampton who had sired three Derby winners in Merry Hampton (1887), Ayrshire (1888) and Ladas (1894). It took 2½ years for the establishment at Egerton House to be completed, with everything on

a grand and extravagant scale: gallops were laid out, belts of sheltering trees planted, the land turned from arable to grass and ranges of stables and boxes built. An innovation was a mile and a quarter moss litter gallop, copied from one Marsh had admired when he had been hunting with the Duc d'Aumale's boarhounds in the forests surrounding Chantilly.

Persimmon made his racecourse début in the Coventry Stakes at Royal Ascot and won convincingly. The Prince of Wales was elated, especially when it was pointed out that Ladas who had won the Derby a fortnight earlier, had been victorious in the Coventry Stakes as a two-year-old. It was a very favourable omen. However, although Persimmon added to his laurels with a victory at Goodwood, the remainder of the season proved disappointing, with the Prince's colt coughing and subsequently being beaten in the Middle Park Stakes by St Frusquin who, like Persimmon, was sired by St Simon. Richard Marsh instinctively knew that Persimmon was the best horse that he had ever trained, but he suffered agonising nightmares at the length of time that the colt took in the spring of 1896 to come to hand. An abscess under one of his teeth did not help his progress, and sadly he was scratched from the Two Thousand Guineas. The Prince confidentially admitted to a friend that Persimmon was so overgrown that he was only half-trained, that he was not fit for the first Classic, and that Marsh was worried as to how to get him ready for the Derby. Yet Marsh, a master of his chosen profession, succeeded in bringing Persimmon to peak condition, although at the eleventh hour disaster nearly struck when Persimmon ignominiously refused to enter the horse-box at Dullingham railway station *en route* for Epsom. Eventually a desperate Marsh offered a sovereign to every bystander who could manhandle the royal colt into the box. This task was carried out with alacrity, leaving Marsh the poorer by many sovereigns, but a much-relieved man.

On Derby Day the imperturbable Jack Watts who had already won three Derbies on Merry Hampton, Sainfoin and Ladas, rode Persimmon a short canter before walking across to The Durdans to inspect some of Lord Rosebery's mares and foals. At 12.30 pm the royal train left Victoria Station, with the party including the Princesses Victoria and Maud of Wales, Prince Charles of Denmark, the Duke and Duchess of York, the Duchess of Teck and the Duke of Cambridge. All were in the happiest of moods, hopeful for Persimmon and wishing the Duke of York 'many happy returns' upon his birthday. On Epsom Downs excitement was pent up, and crowds flocked to booths to see the girl described as 'The Champion High Kicker', the

Derby Day crowds in the early 1900s. (World Graphic Press Ltd)

African and Zulu Exhibition and the young midget boxer who weighed only 3 st 4 lb. There were dwarfs, clowns, acrobats and a fun-fair with merry-go-rounds and swings, 'nigger minstrels', tipsters, pick-pockets, card-sharpers and sellers of ginger-beer all adding to the hustle and bustle, the noise and the hubbub of the occasion.

An hour before the Derby the crowds thronged the paddock to inspect the eleven runners. St Frusquin, who had won the Two Thousand Guineas, was the odds-on favourite and had many admirers, but so, too, had Persimmon, and it was generally agreed that they had the race between them. So it proved, with St Frusquin taking up the running 2 furlongs from home, only to be challenged by Persimmon. Neither horse flinched under the strongest pressure, but the longer-striding Persimmon had the advantage at the line, the judge's verdict being a neck with four lengths between second and third. As the winning number 'ONE' was hoisted into the frame the cheers, like a strong-running tide, surged over the Downs

acclaiming the victory of Persimmon. Yet the reverberating crescendo of cheers were not intended merely to congratulate the Prince upon winning the Derby, for they were also an outward and visible sign of sporting England's regard for the Prince and a tribute to his personal popularity.

The Prince, hat in hand, walked on to the course to greet his champion amidst further roars of approval from the crowd. The grey skies of morning had given way to brilliant sunshine, which seemed appropriate. Marsh, who had hacked back from the start while the race was in progress, could not force his way through the vast throng of spectators, did not see the finish, and only learned the result from jockey Mornington Cannon by the Downs Hotel. The cheering must, however, have given him the easiest and biggest of clues as to the result long before he met Cannon.

Never had such jubilation been witnessed at Epsom and the celebrations were endless. A telegram of congratulation was received from the Queen at Balmoral and in his reply her son stated,

Cartoon by Cecil Aldin, 1901. (Kensington Galleries)

'The scene after the Derby was a most remarkable and gratifying sight.' In the evening the Prince entertained members of the Jockey Club to the annual dinner at Marlborough House. So ended a wonderful day for him, and a historic moment in Derby history. At a later date a statue of Persimmon was erected at the entrance to the Sandringham Stud as a perpetual memorial to a gallant Derby winner.

An interesting sidelight to the Derby appeared in an article published in the *Strand Magazine*:

Mr. R. W. Paul [the photographer] went down a few days before the Derby to make his arrangements. Disappointed in the use of one of the stands, he at length rented a few square yards of ground from a man on the course, whose legal rights were by no means well defined. The spot chosen was near Mr. A. D'Arcy's stand, on the opposite side to the Grand Stand, and about 20yds. past the winning-post. At five o'clock on the morning of Derby Day, Mr. Paul set out for the Downs in a wagonette, with two assistants, and the camera. . . . The inventor paid little heed to the appalling uproar that marked the finish of the race; he only turned his wheel for dear life, and for the benefit of the public who weren't there. The moment the race was over, Mr. Paul whipped out the film, packed it up securely, and made a dash for Epsom Downs station, only regretting that he couldn't take the uproariously

popular sequel to the race—the Prince of Wales leading in his superb horse, Persimmon. However, he had another worry on hand at the moment, for he was by no means sure that his prodigiously long negative was a photographic success. Mr. Paul, I say, left wagonette, camera, assistants, and everything else, and hurried back to London, reaching Hatton Garden at six o'clock. . . . The great negative was developed and hung up to dry at one o'clock in the morning. Later on the Thursday prints were made and tested in the inventor's workshop . . . the same evening an enormous audience at the Alhambra Theatre witnessed the Prince's Derby all to themselves amidst wild enthusiasm, which all but drowned the strains of 'God Bless the Prince of Wales,' as played by the splendid orchestra.

In November 1896 the film, and others made by the enterprising Mr Paul were shown to Queen Victoria at Windsor Castle. Persimmon was undoubtedly a very good three-year-old, certainly far better than Jeddah, also trained by Marsh, who triumphed in the 1898 Derby at 100–1, but probably not the equal of Flying Fox, the Duke of Westminster's 1899 Triple Crown winner. The 1899 Derby and Oaks were the final Epsom Classics to be started by flag, the Derby being marred by the fatal accident to French challenger Holocauste who broke a fetlock and had to be destroyed. Flying Fox was a popular favourite with racegoers, especially after his victory in the Two Thousand Guineas, and on Derby Day London cab-drivers decorated their whips with ribbons in the Westminster colours of yellow and black.

The dawn of the 20th century saw many social and economic changes in Britain, not the least of these changes occuring in horse-racing. The 'American invasion', headed by Tod Sloan, 'Skeets' Martin and later the Reiff brothers, altered the style of jockeyship, and although Sloan was ridiculed for his 'monkey on a stick' style, his success caused others to adopt a similar crouching seat instead of the accepted erect posture with long leathers and a long rein. The Derby was affected by this changing style of jockeyship, and no longer were the first 5 furlongs to the top of Tattenham Corner covered at a comparatively slow pace with the jockeys standing up in the saddle. Due to the Americans the pace from the outset was fast, and proof of the 'wind of change' was that between 1901 and 1906 the record time for the Derby course was lowered on three occasions. A further noticeable change was that the importance, prestige and value of the Derby winner began to increase, with world-wide demands for his services as a stallion. No one doubted the pre-eminence of the Derby as the supreme test of a three-year-old, and as other nations began to establish horse-racing the renown of the Epsom race was steadily enhanced.

The year 1900 gave the Prince of Wales his second Derby victory when Diamond Jubilee, a full brother to Persimmon, won by half a length from Simon Dale. For full brothers to gain immortality at Epsom was remarkable but not unique, for the feat had been achieved by Whalebone and Whisker, both by Waxy out of Penelope, who won in the Duke of Grafton's colours in 1810 and 1815. Diamond Jubilee's triumph was especially appropriate as patriotic fervour was at its height due to the fact that Lord Roberts had only a few more miles to march before entering Johannesburg. Two days after Diamond Jubilee's Derby a telegram was received at Marlborough House:

News of Diamond Jubilee's victory was communicated to me by Stanley during the attack on Brandfort yesterday. Army in South Africa beg to offer respectful congratulations—Roberts.

During the next decade champions in Ard Patrick, Rock Sand, Spearmint and Orby won the Derby which maintained its dramatic record with the defeat of the peerless Sceptre in 1902 when she started an even-money favourite, and a further shock result with the success of 100–1 outsider Signorinetta in 1908. Four years earlier the 'blue jacket, yellow cap' of Mr Leopold de Rothschild was carried to victory by St Amant on an afternoon

when weather conditions were at their very worst. St Amant, his ears stuffed with cotton wool and wearing a hood, took up the running from the start and was never headed. He raced as though the Devil and all the demons of Hell were chasing him, and fear of the thunder and lightning overhead may have lifted his ability to unknown heights. In reality he was not the best colt to contest the race, for this distinction belonged to John O'Gaunt ridden by Mr George Thursby, the outstanding amateur of the era. In the weeks before the race when it became evident that John O'Gaunt must have a chance second to none at Epsom, considerable pressure was brought to bear upon Sir John Thursby who owned the colt, to allow a professional jockey to have the mount at Epsom; but he was adamant that his brother should have the ride. The record books were searched for details of an amateur riding in the Derby, and it was discovered that an Oxford Street bootmaker, Mr Bartley, had ridden Pegasus in the 1837 Derby, a Yorkshire solicitor, Mr Robinson, had ridden his own horse Pelissier in the 1858 Derby, and Mr Bevill had ridden in both the 1862 and 1869 Derbies. Years later Mr Bevill became clerk of the course at Kempton Park. On the eve of St Amant's Derby George Thursby was given a dinner at the Savoy Grill by his brother and some of his friends, but while they wined and dined he merely drank a glass of claret mixed with seltzer. If it had not been for the weather Mr Thursby would probably have won the Derby. Two years later he again rode the runner-up when second on Picton to Spearmint and had his final Derby ride when unplaced on Sir Archibald in 1908.

When Mr Thursby failed on Sir Archibald the heroine was Signorinetta whose owner, Chevalier Ginistrelli, was hardly known to the English racing public. He had arrived from Italy in the 1880s and had set up as a trainer at Newmarket where his activities were not taken seriously by his fellow trainers. His filly had done nothing to indicate that she had the ability to win a Classic although her dam, Signorina, had first-rate credentials. Unbeaten in her nine races, which included the 1889 Middle Park Stakes, she had already produced a top-class colt in Signorino who had been third to Cicero and the luckless French challenger Jardy in the 1905 Derby, so Signorinetta's triumph could not be considered a total fluke.

After the filly passed the post two lengths ahead of the Duke of Portland's Primer, the Chevalier, in a state of wild excitement, rushed on to the course to lead in his heroine. His attire, which included a battered panama hat, did not meet with the approval of many sartorially elegant members in the grandstand, neither did the fact that an outsider with an unfashionable and virtually unknown sire had triumphed, pleased the breeding pundits who hoped that an impeccably bred colt would always succeed in the 'Blue Riband'. However, nothing could dampen the delight of Chevalier Ginistrelli and his exuberance became infectious. Two days later Signorinetta pulverised her opponents in the Oaks, and when King Edward VII led the beaming Chevalier to the front of the royal box, both monarch and Italian owner–breeder–trainer were given a tumultuous reception. For the past 50 years the winning owner, almost without exception, had been a member of the aristocracy—wealthy, affluent and influential. For a slightly comical foreigner, whose English vocabulary was limited, to win the Derby became an unprecedented event.

Primer who finished second to Signorinetta was owned by the Duke of Portland who had already won two Derbies with Ayrshire and Donovan, and in addition had seen his colours carried into second place by Simon Dale and William the Third, and third place by Raeburn, Friar Tuck and now Primer. Master of the Horse in the Royal Household from 1886 to 1892 and from 1895 to 1905, his racing interests were immense. His stallions St Simon, William the Third and the Australian champion Carbine stood at his Welbeck Stud in Nottinghamshire, while Ayrshire and St Serf stood at Egerton House at Newmarket, and Raeburn at the Worksop Manor Stud. He owned more than 50 brood-mares and horses in training, which highlighted the power and the strength of the few racing empires which had dominated the English Turf for so long.

In 1909 the Derby result again proved historic, with Minoru winning in the colours of the King of England, thus providing the only occasion upon which the victor has been owned by the reigning monarch. Minoru had been bred by the eccentric Colonel Hall-Walker, later Lord Wavertree, and leased with five other yearlings bred at his Tully Stud in County Kildare to the King with one of his objects being stated as:

> . . . the value of His Majesty's patronage to the Turf continuing must be apparent to all, and it is essential if he is to continue that patronage that he should enjoy some occasional success . . .

Minoru was sired by Cyllene, probably the best horse of his generation but misguidedly never entered for the Derby, out of Mother Siegel, one of the last mares from the Blankney Stud owned by the King's friend Henry Chaplin. Minoru won the Two Thousand Guineas, and with Bayardo under a cloud, was fully expected to win the Derby although there was strong support for the American-bred colt Sir Martin who had been sold weeks before the race for the huge sum of £15 000.

The royal party, including the Queen who was dressed in her favourite colour of mauve, and the Princess of Wales arrived at Epsom shortly before the first race which was won by a colt ridden by the King's jockey, Herbert Jones. An even better portent came in the second race which was won by a

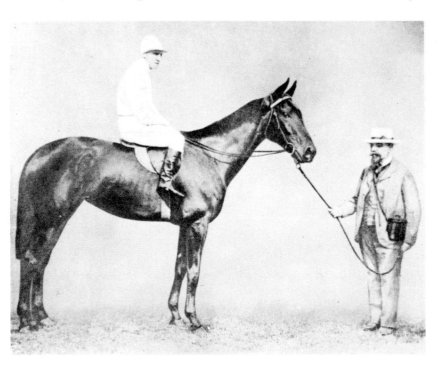

Chevalier E. Ginistrelli with his 1908 Derby heroine Signorinetta (W. Bullock). (Photograph from *Epsom and the Dorlings* by EE Dorling, published by Stanley Paul)

King Edward VII with his 1909 Derby winner Minoru. (*Illustrated London News*)

horse sired by Persimmon. It seemed that events were inexorably leading to the prayed-for, hoped-for Derby result. The Fates must have been at their most generous an hour later, for Minoru triumphed if only by the narrowest margin. A furlong from home Minoru and Louviers were running neck and neck with the race between them. Neither flinched, neither faltered and their two jockeys, Jones and Stern, rode as though inspired. A hundred yards from the post Minoru inched ahead, but Louviers was not yet beaten and reduced the fractional lead by infinitesimal amounts. As the two horses flashed past the post, the pent-up emotion of the crowds which had caused them to cheer vociferously throughout the contest, suddenly slackened into silence and all eyes turned instinctively to the judge's box. Breathlessly they awaited his verdict. 'ONE' was Minoru, and 'ELEVEN' was Louviers. As 'ONE' was hoisted the silence was exchanged for exultant pandemonium which made thousands of spectators dry of throat as the relief from tension turned to sheer jubilation.

The King, obviously overcome by the reception awarded him, came to the entrance to the winner's enclosure to greet Minoru who was being mobbed in a sea of spectators. Ever courteous and considerate the King was heard to remark, 'Please do not touch him or he may kick.' Enthusiasts, forgetful of the Royal personage, slapped him on the back and it is claimed that one staunch Tory had the

temerity to say, 'Your Majesty, now you have won the Derby, go home and sack the Government.'

In 1910, when Lemberg won the Derby the royal box was closed, and the Union Jack, instead of the Royal Standard, flew above the private stand. Many racegoers wore black armbands in memory of their beloved King Edward VII, and the occasion was sombre in the extreme. Third to Lemberg was Charles O'Malley ridden by a young jockey having his first Derby mount. The jockey's name, chalked on the number-boards, was Steve Donoghue. He was to be third again, riding Royal Tender, in 1911, did not have a mount in 1912 when the filly Tagalie gave her sporting owner Mr Walter Raphael compensation for his disappointment when his colt Louviers had been so narrowly beaten by Minoru, and in 1913 rode Bachelor's Wedding in the most controversial Derby in memory.

Due to wartime conditions a New Derby was run over the July course at Newmarket from 1915 to 1918, and part of the Epsom grandstand became a hospital for wounded soldiers. Only in 1919 did the 'Blue Riband' return to Epsom where its subsequent six years' history was inseparably linked with the name and the fame of Donoghue who had ridden Pommern and Gay Crusader to victory in Newmarket Derbies, and was now to ride four Epsom Derby winners and become a national hero as admired as 'The Tinman' had been. In 1921 he won on Humorist and was to follow this success

Lord Woolavington's Coronach, 1926 Derby hero with jockey J. Childs, by Lynwood Palmer.
(The Jockey Club, Newmarket)

with victories on Captain Cuttle (1922), Papyrus (1923) and Manna (1925). He could have added further to this impressive list if he had not infuriated Lord Woolavington, thus depriving himself of the mount on Coronach.

Captain Cuttle, a massive chestnut colt with a white face, white forelegs and a white near hind sock, was trained at Beckhampton by Fred Darling for whisky magnate Lord Woolavington who had been raised to the peerage earlier in the year. He had wished to be known as Lord Buchanan but was unable to take this title as it belonged to the Dukes of Montrose. Captain Cuttle was second in the Two Thousand Guineas, ridden by Vic Smyth, but Donoghue, now riding free-lance, had set his sights upon having the mount at Epsom. Complications ensued, but after some telephone calls, and a flight by Donoghue to Beckhampton to ride Captain Cuttle in an exercise gallop and Darling's refusal to allow him to do so as he had not obtained the owner's permission, it was announced that 'Steve'

and not Smyth would ride Captain Cuttle in the Derby.

Derby Day was one of the hottest of the century, and the huge crowd sizzled in the heat. One onlooker noted that there were 'fat women in purple satin with ostrich feathers in their bonnets, and babies galore in traps with their fathers blowing cornets and drinking stout . . . blue clouds of petrol fumes contaminating the air . . . and trees bandaged with posters advertising soap, newspapers, and chocolate, and giving news of the execution of the poisoner Armstrong. . . .'

Lord Woolavington, whose Derby runners had been fourth in both the 1920 and 1921 races, was hoping for better luck, as was Lord Astor who had crossed the Atlantic hoping that his frustrating record of 'seconditis' with Blink (1918), Buchan (1919) and Craig-an-Eran (1921) would be broken, and that his much-fancied colt Tamar would succeed where they had failed. For the first time in Derby history the runners carried numbered saddle-

Right: Lord Woolavington's Captain Cuttle, 1922, by Lynwood Palmer (S. Donoghue). (The Jockey Club, Newmarket)

Cartoon of Jockey Club Members, 1927, by The Tout. (The Jockey Club, Newmarket)

cloths as they paraded in the paddock. When the horses left the paddock Donoghue discovered to his horror that Captain Cuttle was lame, and precious, agonising minutes were wasted in suspense after the jockey had dismounted and noticed that one of Captain Cuttle's plates was broken. No blacksmith could be found, and a distraught Fred Darling began to wonder if the race would start without Lord Woolavington's colt. Eventually all was well, and as Steve took Captain Cuttle to the start, the vast crowd on the Downs poured more money into the bookmakers' satchels supporting their hero, for without question the masses of holidaying spectators had blind faith in the ability of Steve and would have backed his mount even it it had been a donkey. Curiously there were 13 letters in the words 'Captain Cuttle', 'Steve Donoghue', and 'James Buchanan' and even more curious and far fetched was the fact that the date 31.5.22 added up to 13. This may have appealed to the superstitious, but literary-minded racegoers were adamant that Captain Cuttle could not win as he was named after the Dickens character 'Cap'n Cuttle' in *Dombey and Son*, and no colt could triumph in the Derby if his name was spelt incorrectly.

As 'They're Off' reverberated throughout the grandstands one American visitor noted the occasion and later wrote:

> The roar of a great crowd is a wonderful noise, it seems to have as many distinct sounds in it as Niagara. If you can hear the sea in it, you can also hear the Carillon of Bruges and a hooting of steamships on the Banks, and I believe no crowd, not even a New York baseball crowd at a great baseball match roars so long and so loud as the Derby Day thousands roar.

Moments later, or to be precise 2 minutes ·34$\frac{3}{5}$ seconds later, Steve had won by four lengths, becoming the first jockey since Danny Maher in

1905 and 1906 to win in consecutive years. News of Captain Cuttle's victory was telegraphed across the world and was known in Australia less than 3 minutes after the race was won. This was a new telegraphic achievement for the previous best time was 12 minutes. In the evening Steve celebrated his victory by giving a dinner-party at Prince's Restaurant, Piccadilly, before taking some of his fellow jockeys to Daly's Theatre. In a newspaper article George Duller, famed as a hurdle jockey, wrote:

> The reason why Donoghue always distinguished himself at Epsom is that he is so clever at getting off and gets going so well that he is rarely if ever bunched in going downhill. In the recent Derbies we had proof of this. Neither Captain Cuttle nor Humorist had any trouble through the interference of other horses, while Abbot's Trace was so far clear of his field that he would have won the Derby if he had not collapsed when leading. Donoghue knows every inch of the track at Epsom and his presence on a horse is the equivalent to lightening the animal's weight by at least 7 lb. . . . .

When the time came for Steve to choose his 1923 Derby mount he again behaved with the anticipated and typical 'wriggling and writhing' towards his retainer with Lord Woolavington. He had no desire to ride any horse in the Derby save Papyrus, owned by Mr Ben Irish, and made his desire blatantly obvious. Lord Woolavington, justifiably indignant, told the jockey exactly what he thought of him, gave him a lecture on loyalty and integrity, and cancelled his retainer, announcing that Donoghue would never ride for him again. Despite this altercation, the all-important fact emerged that Steve would ride Papyrus whose length victory over Pharos, owned by Lord Derby, gave the incorrigible jockey the unique achievement of three consecutive Derby victories. In the first race on the afternoon of Derby Day Steve had been hit by a flying stone and returned to the weighing-room almost blinded in his left eye. A raw beefsteak was procured and temporarily put over the eye which might have been permanently lost if the flint had struck a fraction higher.

The year 1924 not only broke Steve's sequence, but brought success for the first time in 137 years to a colt racing in the colours of an Earl of Derby. The afternoon was one of the wettest ever recorded, and the rain so heavy that long before the end of the afternoon the course was not fit for racing. Sansovino, ridden by Tommy Weston and trained by the Hon George Lambton, was the only horse to revel

'The Yellow Earl'—Lord Lonsdale riding his hack down the course at Epsom in 1924 to inspect the ground badly damaged by torrential rain, (Charles Langlands)

A coach and four arriving at Epsom on Derby Day, 1930. (Syndication International Ltd)

in the 'Passchendaele' conditions which had turned the track into a quagmire, and stormed home to win by six lengths from St Germans, owned by the still luckless Lord Astor. An hour after the Derby Tommy Weston was riding a wooden horse on a merry-go-round on the Downs unrecognised by the crowds sheltering from the appalling weather. In consequence of the rain causing such havoc to the race-track the Jockey Club demanded that certain alterations were carried out, including improvements to the grandstand accommodation. To comply with Jockey Club edicts, firstly the freehold of Epsom Downs was bought on behalf of the Epsom Grandstand Association from the Trustees of the Lord of the Manor. To pay for this purchase the Walton Manor estate training grounds were sold to trainer Stanley Wootton for £35 000. It was also decided to raise £100 000 additional capital in order to rebuild the grandstand completely. The work of demolition commenced a fortnight after the 1926 Derby, but the General Strike caused delays

and increased costs. It needed the inspiration of Lord Lonsdale who organised a dinner for all the workmen to induce the needed redoubling of effort so that the new grandstand was finished by Derby Day 1927.

Two years earlier Steve Donoghue had resumed his victorious way, winning on Manna, owned by Shanghai bill broker Mr H E Morriss. At the annual Press Club luncheon presided over by Edgar Wallace, who had arranged the first of these lunches in 1923 during his presidential year of office, the famous author of thrillers remarked: 'We are on the eve of a Derby so open that it resembles one of those November selling plates, when every horse is trying and nobody is betting.' When Mr Morriss was called upon to speak he wittily commented: 'The reason why the Israelites found themselves in the rich and fertile plains of the Jordan was that they followed manna. My advice to you is to do the same.' Mr Morriss was followed by Lord Birkenhead who pointed out that when an owner with a

Mid-day Sun—being led in by Mrs G. Miller, the first woman owner of an Epsom Derby winner. (*Illustrated London News*)

fancied Derby candidate claimed 'May the best horse win' he really meant 'May my horse be the best.' At the same lunch it was pointed out that the man who owns the favourite for the Derby is entrusted with a great responsibility; from the day that his horse wins its first race the public acquires a right in the animal.

Derby Day was again marred by heavy rain, yet such conditions may have prevented an ugly scene, for four rival gangs—the Aldersgate Boys, the Birmingham Boys, the Clerkenwell Gang and the Hatton Garden Gang—had threatened to settle their differences by pitched battle on the Downs during Derby Day. There were more than 1000 police on duty, but the weather was so atrocious that 'a thousand lifeboatmen in cork belts and sou'westers would have been better'. As Donoghue unconcernedly cantered to the start on Manna, he had a writ for money owed to a money-lender by a third party but guaranteed by him, stuffed into the top of his breeches. The writ had been handed to him as he left the paddock, and it remained in his breeches throughout the race which he won by eight lengths to give him his easiest Derby victory. News of Manna's success was learned in the House of Commons in an ingenious manner when a Member, having seen the result on the tape machine, marched

April the Fifth (F. Lane), the 1932 hero, with his owner Mr Tom Walls. (*The British Racehorse*)

Left: Spectators on the Downs watching a 'Houdini' rope trick, 1967. (Syndication International Ltd)

Centre: Derby contestants parading in the paddock under the critical eyes of owners and trainers, 1973. (Syndication International Ltd)

Bottom left: Open-topped buses arriving on the Downs on Derby Day 1974. (Syndication International Ltd).

Below: The irrepressible Ras Prince Monolulu (Syndication International Ltd)

Her Majesty the Queen and His Royal Highness the
Duke of Edinburgh talking to newly knighted Gordon
Richards before the 1953 Derby. (Syndication
International Ltd)

Never the easiest of men with whom to deal, he was
ruthless, devoid of compassion, hated mediocrity,
and was a martinet where stable discipline was
concerned. He frequently wandered around the
stable yard in the evening, wearing gym shoes in
order to catch lazy and indolent stablemen. No
trainer has ever turned out his horses looking more
immaculate. The best horse that he trained was
Hurry On who did not run in the Derby but sired
Captain Cuttle and Coronach. He also sired Call
Boy who won the 1927 Derby in the colours of the
dying theatrical impresario Frank Curzon.

The 1927 Derby found the new grandstand in use,
and in addition the BBC gave the first running
commentary upon the race—with the race-reader
Geoffrey Gilbey and the paddock expert George
Alison. Derby Day was also unusual in that the
Midday Standard, who had exclusive rights to Steve
Donoghue's opinion, arranged for a fleet of Moth
aeroplanes to fly over London and by means of a
series of lights give his tip for the Derby in a code
known only to the paper's readers.

A year after Call Boy's victory Lord Derby was
robbed of another Derby success when Fairway, the
best three-year-old in the kingdom, lost his chance
long before the race started. Fairway, the 3–1
favourite, was senselessly and thoughtlessly mobbed by countless well-wishers as he left the paddock,
had hairs plucked from his tail and took such fright
that all hope of success had vanished before the
sweating unnerved colt reached his rivals at the
start, and he finished in the ruck behind Felstead.
Weeks after Felstead's victory Edgar Wallace was
visiting Lord Dewar's stud farm. As the two men
admired the mares and foals the host remarked:
'That colt will win the Derby, if I am alive
to see it.' The colt was Cameronian and as his
breeding and merits were acclaimed Lord Dewar
mentioned the Jockey Club 'Void Nomination' rule
under which the death of an owner after a
nomination had been made and prior to the running
of the race, automatically caused the cancellation of
the nomination. The reason for the rule was the
belief that the Jockey Club could not recover entry
fees and forfeits from executors by legal process.
The rule had recently resulted in the very useful colt
Midlothian forfeiting his Derby engagement due to
the death of Lord Rosebery.

Edgar Wallace decided, having talked to Lord
Dewar, to challenge the Jockey Club rule which he
thought was outmoded. In broad outline the Jockey
Club were also unhappy and were convinced that

into the Chamber and solemnly asked the sup-
plementary question: 'Is the House aware that
Manna has won the Derby?' Strangely the Derby
result had a Middle East flavour, for Manna had
Biblical overtones, the second horse was Zionist,
and the third was The Sirdar, the name given to the
Military Commander of the Egyptian Army.
Understandably, Donoghue was fêted after every
newspaper carried eulogies while examining his life
story. One of the wisest comments was:

> There is a physical as well as spiritual side to Steve's
> success. It is called balance. Watch him come down
> the Hill at Epsom. You never see him holding on to
> the reins as many of his colleagues are compelled to.
> His touch is as light downhill as it is on the flat, and
> that I believe is why he is so successful on the Downs
> course. His mounts have never any shifting dead
> weight to carry. . . .

Fred Darling, who trained both Captain Cuttle
and Manna, was to send out his third Derby winner
when Coronach won in 1926 for Lord Woolavington. Although Darling had ridden a few winners as
an apprentice, he had never held a jockey's licence.
His father had trained both Galtee More and Ard
Patrick at Beckhampton where Fred took over
shortly after returning from Germany in 1912.

The arrival of the Royal Party for the Coronation Derby, 1953. (Fox Photos Ltd)

Pinza four lengths ahead of Aureole at the finish of the Coronation Year Derby. (Sport and General)

Walking to the paddock—Her Majesty the Queen with the Duke of Norfolk, to inspect the Derby contestants in 1967—the year of Royal Palace. (Syndication International Ltd)

the rule was unreasonable, but their legal advisers maintained that it was not legally possible for the rule to be altered. However, Edgar Wallace was fired with enthusiasm, entered one of his many indifferent horses for a minor race, and deliberately refused to pay the paltry forfeit of £4 which he owed. He then invited the Jockey Club to sue him. At the first hearing Mr Justice Clauson ruled that racing entrance fees were part of a contract by way of gaming and wagering and, therefore, came under the Gaming Act of 1845 and were not recoverable by law. This caused consternation, but on appeal, to the delight of all parties, this verdict was reversed, Wallace paid his £4 and the Jockey Club promptly deleted 'The Void Nomination' rule and reimbursed the playwright's costs. Lord Dewar died in April 1930, and in consequence his brilliant, unbeaten colt Challenge was not able to run in the 1930 Derby won by Blenheim, but the entry for Cameronian remained valid with the happiest of results in June 1931 when he won the Derby, ridden by F. Fox and trained by Fred Darling.

As the 1920s ended, with Donoghue's star no longer in the ascendant, the Derby became influenced and to a large extent dominated by HH Aga Khan whose first hint of Epsom glory had been when his 'chocolate and green' colours had been carried by Zionist. In 1930 his colt Blenheim had

Tension and excitement reach their zenith as the runners are about to leave the starting stalls. (Syndication International Ltd)

Mr HJ Joel's Royal Palace, 1967, by Richard Stone Reeves. (The Jockey Club, Newmarket)

brought him his first Derby on a day when a totalisator operated for the first time at Epsom. During the next 7 years his colt Dastur finished second to April the Fifth, Bahram won in 1935, and the following year he had the excitement of owning not only the winner Mahmoud but also the runner-up Taj Akbar, while Le Grand Duc was third to Mrs GB Miller's Mid-day Sun in 1937, when the result was historic in that it was the first occasion in Epsom Derby history that the winner had carried the colours of a woman. To add to women's glory on that memorable afternoon the runner-up Sandsprite was both owned and trained by Mrs Florence Nagle, although her head-lad held the licence.

Interspersed with the Derby dominance of HH Aga Khan in the 1930s were victories achieved by Hyperion and Windsor Lad, both of whom were supremely great thoroughbreds, and the success of April the Fifth, a colt of more modest pretensions who may have benefited by good fortune as King

George V's Limelight—a very useful horse—had never been entered for the Derby. The day after April the Fifth won at Epsom his owner–trainer, Tom Walls, who was better known as an actor, film star and bon viveur, wrote:

> . . . no thrill can ever again match that of last Wednesday afternoon shortly after three o'clock when April the Fifth went past the post. I was bemused. I know not what I said, what I did. I am told that I did not cheer—I laughed aloud and then raced for the stairs . . . just a few seconds before my horse passed the post I gave up hope. I saw him, seemingly hemmed in, without room to make his effort. I know I said aloud 'it is hopeless' and my glasses turned to the duel between Dastur and Miracle—I deserted my horse. Then suddenly I heard someone cry 'What is that pink capped thing on the outside?' IT WAS MINE!

In the final 2 years before the Second World War the Derby was won by top-class colts in Bois

Roussel and Blue Peter who carried Lord Rosebery's colours to a convincing victory over Fox Club and Heliopolis. The 1938 Derby had been the first televised by the BBC, and the success of the operation resulted in further television coverage in Blue Peter's year.

For the next 6 years the Epsom grandstand stood gaunt and forlorn, with the Prince's stand used as an officers' mess. Luckily no immense damage was caused by the bombs of enemy aircraft indiscriminately jettisoning their loads of death, but one bomb exploded in Tattersalls' enclosure. In 1946, however, the Derby returned from the July course at Newmarket to its rightful home. There was an atmosphere of austerity about the scene on Wednesday, 5 June, and although King George VI and Queen Elizabeth were present, there was none of the pre-war smartness about the occasion. The grandstands needed repainting, there were no top hats to be seen, and for every civilian there was at least one racegoer in uniform.

It would have been a sensational and appropriate return to Epsom if the first post-war Derby could have fallen to a colt carrying the famous 'black, white cap' of Lord Derby, but his candidate Gulf Stream, a son of Hyperion, was beaten a length by the unconsidered 50–1 outsider Airborne who became only the fourth grey to win, following in the footsteps of Gustavus, Tagalie and Mahmoud.

The next 6 years saw two more victories for HH Aga Khan with My Love and Tulyar, and the Derby run on a Saturday instead of the traditional

St Paddy, the 1960 Derby winner. (T R H Neame)

Wednesday in 1947, 1948 and 1949 by order of the Government—and to the disgust of Charles Langlands who had been clerk of the course since 1926 and Managing Director of the Epsom Grandstand Association since 1944. French successes were scored with Pearl Diver and Galcador, and a result which gladdened the heart of all National Hunt enthusiasts occurred in 1951 when Arctic Prince, trained by Willie Stephenson, won from Sybil's Nephew and Signal Box, ridden by Martin Molony. One of the closest finishes in the history of the Derby had occurred 2 years previously when Nimbus beat Amour Drake by a head with Lord Derby's Swallow Tail a further neck away third. The photo-finish camera was used by the judge for the first time to determine the result; and inevitably, without disparaging the decisions given in close finishes in the past, one must wonder if

Eighteen-year-old Lester Piggott winning his first Derby on Never Say Die, owned by American Mr Robert Sterling Clark, 1954. (Syndication International Ltd)

Dr Carlo Vittadini enters the unsaddling enclosure with his 1975 Derby winner Grundy ridden by Pat Eddery. (Syndication International Ltd)

the camera, had it been in existence, would have failed to endorse the verdict decided upon by the judge.

Coronation Year brought victory, after years and years of disappointment and frustration, to newly knighted Sir Gordon Richards. Born in 1904, he had ridden his first winner in 1921 and without question was the most popular jockey of the era, with a reputation for integrity which was never dented by a blemish of any sort. Yet despite his brilliant success, with 13 Classic victories to his credit, he had failed to ride a Derby winner in 27 attempts since his first ride, on Skyflight, in Sansovino's year. It was as though an Epsom jinx overshadowed him, and while there were those who claimed that his impetuosity was the cause of his failure, he did not ride a colt with an outstanding chance until he partnered Manitoba in 1933. The following year he finished second on Easton to Windsor Lad, and in 1936 elected to ride Taj Akbar who was more fancied than HH Aga Khan's other runner Mahmoud. Two years later he started a hot favourite on Pasch, owned by Mr H E Morriss, but

Lester Piggott. (David Hastings)

Greville Starkey forces Shirley Heights into the lead to defeat Hawaiian Sound in the 1978
Derby. (Syndication International Ltd)

could only manage to finish third to Bois Roussel
and Scottish Union, while in 1939 he again rode the
runner-up, Fox Club. During the war years he
missed a winning ride on Owen Tudor due to a
broken leg, and the next year his mount Big Game
failed to stay the trip. In 1943 Nasrullah refused to
exert himself despite all the champion jockey's
persuasion, and 4 years later at Epsom he found
that Tudor Minstrel, 7–4-on favourite, had run out
of speed and stamina long before Pearl Diver,
Migoli and Sayajirao had passed him. Such misery
would have totally disheartened men of lesser
character, but not Gordon Richards who, like
Robert the Bruce, was prepared to try and try and
try again.

At long last came his moment of deserved glory.
He had taken a house at Worthing for Derby Week,
as was his custom each year. On Saturday, 6 June,
he rode Pinza at exercise before breakfasting at
George Duller's house where he attempted to rest
and relax. Enormous crowds had thronged to
Epsom and patriotism, already at fever pitch, was
further heightened by the fact that Her Majesty's

Aureole was thought to have a great chance of
victory. Yet in the race nothing had the remotest
chance with Pinza who won by four lengths. In his
autobiography Sir Gordon Richards wrote:

> . . . I have been told that my expression never
> changed, that I seemed to take that tremendous
> moment unnaturally quietly, even when I was being
> led in. This seems to have surprised some people, in
> view of the fact that I had just won my first Derby
> after all those years of disappointment. But I am not
> surprised myself. Frankly my mind was in a turmoil,
> and my brain perhaps a little numbed. Everyone was
> being so tremendously kind. . . .

Twelve months later another historic Derby
triumph was achieved when American-bred and
-owned Never Say Die won in the hands of 18-year-
old Lester Piggott who became the youngest rider of
an Epsom Derby winner in the 20th century. His
grandfather, Ernest Piggott, had ridden two Grand
National winners, and married Margaret Cannon
whose brothers Mornington and Kempton had
both ridden Derby winners, succeeding on Flying
Fox and St Amant. Lester's father, Keith Piggott,

was a first-class steeplechase jockey and his mother a member of the Rickaby family. No one has ever been more suitably bred for his chosen profession, and few were surprised when Lester rode his first winner at the age of 13, especially when it was appreciated that his great-grandfather had ridden the winner of the 1882 Derby and one of his great-great-uncles, Sam Day, had ridden the Derby winners of 1821, 1830 and 1846, while another great-great-uncle had trained Pyrrhus the First, Cossack and Andover.

Before his victory on Never Say Die Lester had already been second on Gay Time to Tulyar in the 1952 Derby, and had partnered the unplaced Prince Charlemagne in the Coronation Derby. Since 1954 Lester's name has been synonymous with the Derby—and indeed all Classics—and despite the claims of Archer and Donoghue it is Piggott who emerges as the greatest Derby jockey of the past two centuries. Totally dedicated, his victories on Crepello (1957), St Paddy (1960), Sir Ivor (1968), Nijinsky (1970), Roberto (1972), Empery (1976) and The Minstrel (1977) are a permanent reminder of his brilliance, artistry and supreme skill. There has never been a better judge of pace, no greater student of the form book, no stronger finisher when ice-cool judgement, nerve and determination to

make his mount give his all, are desperately needed in the final strides before the winning-post is reached.

In Noel Murless, knighted in 1976, and Vincent O'Brien he has been fortunate to find two trainers whose ability bordered on genius, and whose skill in producing their Epsom hopes at peak condition on the afternoon of Derby Day has brought them the admiration of the racing world. Yet Piggott's career as a Derby jockey has not been meteoric, and for more than 25 years he has consistently been 'the star', although at times his behaviour has been reminiscent of that of Steve Donoghue, and his replacement of W. Williamson on Roberto in 1972 at almost the eleventh hour, did not enhance his reputation. The reason for the 'switch' was supposedly Williamson's ill-health, yet the Australian rode the winner of a race at Epsom later on the afternoon of Derby Day.

The year after Piggott won on St Paddy, a shock result occurred when the 66–1 outsider Psidium, trained by Harry Wragg, beat Dicta Drake by two lengths, with Pardao a neck away third. An unusual feature of the result was that all three colts were owned by women—Mrs Arpad Plesch, Mme Leon Volterra and Mrs CO Iselin. Few of the bookmakers on the Downs laid Psidium, but one who did

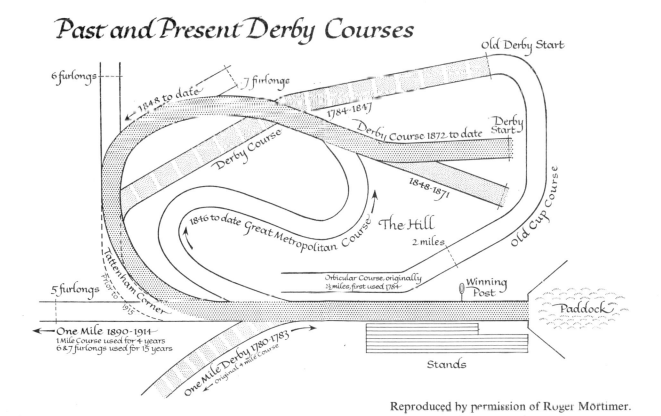

Past and Present Derby Courses

Reproduced by permission of Roger Mortimer.

so to a large amount asked the lucky punter: 'Why did you back the winner?' The reply, 'Because I was on a cruiser of that name during the war,' invoked the angry reply from the aggrieved bookmaker, 'Pity it was not the *Titanic*.'

During the past three decades Epsom racecourse has endured many administrative vicissitudes and improvements. The Rosebery stand has been built, the freehold of the 9-acre paddock purchased from The Durdans estate, and a new single-storey block of stables with 100 boxes and sleeping accommodation for 90 stable-lads and 20 stable-girls constructed. The condition of the track has come in for severe criticism from many experienced jockeys and pressmen, and a pedestrian tunnel has been built under the course, while attempts have been made to prevent gipsies from monopolising the Downs during Derby Week. Charles Langlands retired in 1954 and was succeeded by John Watts who resigned in favour of Major Peter Beckwith-Smith 10 years later. Nothing, however, was more important where the future of Epsom racecourse is concerned than the munificent offer of the 206 acres of the Walton Downs gallops made by Mr Stanley Wootton in April 1969 to the Levy Board 'at the rent of a peppercorn if demanded'. The Levy Board Chairman Lord Wigg accepted this and immediately began negotiations to acquire Epsom Downs in addition, by bidding 30 shillings for each 10 shilling-share in United Racecourses (formed by the merger of Epsom Grandstand Association and Sandown Park Ltd), the total bid amounting to £1·359 million. The take-over was duly ratified in

July 1969, and within 6 months a board of management was formed to maintain the Epsom and Walton Downs gallops. Various involved Local Government Acts can affect the issue in future years, but in broad outline, due to the generosity of Mr Wootton and the perspicacity of Lord Wigg, Epsom racecourse belongs to the nation in perpetuity.

A highlight in the history of the Derby occurred in 1973 with the victory of Morston who, like the 1969 hero Blakeney, was out of the mare Windmill Girl. Morganette and Perdita II are the only other mares to have had the distinction of producing two Derby winners during the past 100 years, but whereas Persimmon and Diamond Jubilee were full brothers, Galtee More and Ard Patrick, and Blakeney and Morston were half-brothers. However, the triumph of Windmill Girl's sons brought a further Derby record since Arthur Budgett became only the second man to have bred, owned and trained two Derby winners. This outstanding feat had been achieved previously by William I'Anson with Blink Bonny and her son Blair Athol in 1857 and 1864.

Since Morston's victory the Derby heroes have been Snow Knight, Grundy, Empery, The Minstrel and Shirley Heights who has been retired to the Royal Stud at Sandringham. In future years a Derby victory by a colt sired by Shirley Heights out of a mare owned by Her Majesty the Queen would add further glory to the 'Blue Riband of the Turf' which is deservedly acknowledged as a part of Britain's heritage.

SECTION 2

Sensational and dramatic Derbies

The scandal of Running Rein 1844

Villainy on the Turf reached the depths of nefarious skulduggery in 1844 when the four-year-old Running Rein was first past the post in the Derby and subsequently disqualified after an investigation and a court case which would have made a modern detective story seem second rate! The drama was the culmination of the crimes, substitutions, deceptions and swindles which had beset racing since the end of the Napoleonic Wars, and with the condemnation of the perpetrators of the Running Rein fraud and their guilt conclusively proved, racing entered a new era of respectability.

The complicated and involved Running Rein fraud began in September 1841 when Abraham Levi Goodman, who lived in Foley Place, London, and was a quick-witted unscrupulous villain, bought a yearling at Tattersall's Doncaster Sales. The astute and plausible Goodman spent much of his life scheming betting *coups* and would go to any lengths in his efforts to bring them to fruition. A month after he had bought the yearling to whom the name 'Maccabeus' was given, Goodman bought a colt

foal for 28 gns as the second act of his deep-rooted plot. The following spring the foal, now a yearling and called Running Rein, arrived at stables in Langham Place, London from Yorkshire, where he had been bred by Dr Cobb, a Malton surgeon, from whom a local trainer, Harry Stebbings, had bought Running Rein on behalf of Goodman and kept him throughout the winter months. The Langham Place area abounded with stables and the small dwellings of grooms and horse-dealers, and the arrival of the yearling passed unnoticed.

No one will ever know the precise moment at which Levi Goodman decided to win the 1844 Derby with a four-year-old masquerading as a three-year-old; but it was almost certainly before October 1842 when three colts, including Maccabeus and Running Rein, were taken by Goodman to William Smith, an Epsom trainer who requested the vastly experienced George Hitchcock to break them in. Many years later Hitchcock admitted that although Goodman told him that all three colts were yearlings, it did cross his mind that one of them

Running Rein, who was disqualified after winning the 1844 Derby, by J. Rogers Sen. (Fores Gallery, London)

Maccabeus was sufficiently developed to be a year older. However, he was frightened of Smith, and when, on a previous occasion he had tentatively queried the age of a horse, Smith had lost his temper and horse-whipped him.

At this moment the saga becomes more involved than ever—Goodman was determined that Maccabeus should impersonate Running Rein, and thus should be contesting two-year-old races in 1843 and three-year-old races in 1844. But the 1843 season was still 6 months away and what, thought the wily Goodman, would happen if anyone appreciated the deception by realising the 'switch'. If neither colt ran until 1844 questions were certain to be asked as to what had happened to Maccabeus, and questions were the last thing required by Goodman. As a part of his master-plan, therefore, he went to Ireland and bought a two-year-old who impersonated Maccabeus throughout the early part of the 1843 racing season! During the summer, after the Irish colt had impersonated Maccabeus, he disappeared and it was given out that Maccabeus was dead. Nothing more was done until October when the genuine

Maccabeus ran in a two-year-old race at Newmarket under the name 'Running Rein'. Not surprisingly he won, for he was a year older than his opponents—but the object of Goodman's plan was that observers at Newmarket would recognise the *same* colt when they saw him in the paddock at Epsom 8 months later. To make this task easier both colts, Maccabeus and Running Rein, were scarred to make them look more alike, for the eventual moment when the genuine Running Rein took the place of the impostor.

One man, Lord George Bentinck, was already very dubious about the activities of Goodman, He was exceedingly suspicious of 'Running Rein' owing to rumours which he had heard, and the belief that the horse he saw at Newmarket looked too big and won too impressively to be a two-year-old. He insisted that the Newmarket stewards hold an inquiry, but although they agreed to do so, a fortnight elapsed before the inquiry was held. This 14-day respite saved Goodman, for if the horse which won at Newmarket had been examined immediately someone would undoubtedly have claimed that it was a three-year-old. In the event when one of Dr Cobb's young grooms was brought from Malton a fortnight later to identify the horse, he saw the genuine Running Rein and not Maccabeus. The groom's identification was positive, but, of course, he never realised that the horse he had identified was not the one which had run at Newmarket, but rather the colt which had been bred by Dr Cobb. Goodman had outwitted the Jockey Club, much to the indignation of Lord George Bentinck. All that remained before the 1844 Derby was to wager as much money as possible upon 'Running Rein'.

The Derby was due to be run on Wednesday, 22 May, and to confuse the issue still further Goodman had sold 'Running Rein' to an innocent Mr Wood. However, to Goodman's consternation the previous Saturday a protest against Running Rein, signed by Lord George Bentinck, John Bowes and John Scott, was sent to the Epsom stewards, and also announced at Tattersalls. The protest took the form of a letter stating that in the opinion of the authors Running Rein was not a three-year-old. To Bentinck's undisguised fury the stewards did nothing other than announce that should Running Rein win, then further investigations might be made. Goodman's plot, however, was now at its zenith. It was to his dismay that he saw, in the parade-ring on Derby Day, the farmer who had wintered Maccabeus in 1842 shaking his head in disbelief and amazement as though in recognition of the four-year-old. By another ironic twist of fate one of the Derby runners, Croton Oil, was out of the same mare as Maccabeus and owned by Lord George Bentinck. Nevertheless, it seemed that Goodman could not fail.

The race proved uneventful, except for Leander's fatal accident, with Running Rein winning by three-quarters of a length from Colonel Peel's Orlando. What was not uneventful was that within an hour Colonel Peel, a member of the Jockey Club and brother of Sir Robert Peel, Prime Minister in 1834

and 1841, had been persuaded to lodge an objection to the winner.

In the days which followed the Derby Lord George Bentinck left no stone unturned in his efforts to bring Goodman to justice. He went to Ireland and saw Thomas Ferguson who had sold Goodman the colt who impersonated Maccabeus; he went to Malton to see Dr Cobb, and he arranged for investigators to make discreet inquiries in the Langham Place area. In reality, however, there was more to Bentinck's industry than the pursuit of the truth. He was hell-bent upon revenge and nothing was too much trouble in his efforts to discredit Goodman—even infamy on his own part. Suddenly, as clear as daylight, he saw the loophole by which Goodman could escape and equally the manner in which he could trump Goodman's ace, even if he had to cheat or revoke to do so. When the case was heard, everything would hinge on Running Rein being produced for inspection. Goodman would obviously cause the disappearance of the four-year-old Maccabeus and produce the real three-year-old Running Rein, swearing that this was the colt who had won the Derby. There was only one way to prevent this—and Bentinck took it. He caused the genuine three-year-old Running Rein to be spirited away from the Epsom stables where he was lodged.

The case, Wood v Peel, was heard by Baron Alderson, a keen racing enthusiast, and a special jury on 1 July 1844 at the Court of Exchequer at Westminster. After 2 days of evidence had been given before a crowded court, with the judge continually demanding 'Produce the horse', the plaintiff's case collapsed. Cockburn, Wood's counsel, more or less threw in his hand, Wood withdrew from the case and the judge returned a verdict for the defendant. Goodman had fled to France before the trial ended, the Jockey Club publicly thanked Lord George Bentinck for the immense service he had rendered to racing, and Orlando was awarded the Derby.

The ruin of the Marquess of Hastings 1867 and 1868

Two of the most tragic Derbies were those of 1867 and 1868, for the results spelled financial ruin for the young, dissolute 4th Marquess of Hastings. It was his misfortune to have been born a hundred years too late, for as a rake and a reckless gambler he was totally out of place amidst the new morality of Victorian England, whereas his life-style would have been accepted and approved by the Regency Bucks who would have understood his overriding desire for popularity, adulation and the excitement that only gambling can bring.

Henry, 4th and last Marquess of Hastings, was born on 22 July 1842. His father died less than 2 years later, and the sudden unexpected death of his elder brother in 1851 brought him an enormous inheritance centred upon the estates of Donington Hall, a vast Gothic mansion on the borders of Leicestershire and Derbyshire. By the time that Hastings attained his majority after spending some of his youth at Eton and Oxford, his estates were valued at more than £250 000 and provided him with an income of £20 000 a year. Yet within 6 years he was dead, his estates sold to pay for his extravagances and his gambling debts, hundreds of thousands of which were incurred over the Derbies of 1867 and 1868. No man has lost more upon the Turf in so short a space of time, and his ruin heralded the commencement of a more virtuous era in the history of racing.

Soon after his 21st birthday Hastings was elected to the Jockey Club, but the social prestige that this bestowed did not preclude his enjoyment of the brothels, hells, cockpits and dens of vice of the East End of London where the toast 'The Markis— Gawd bless 'im' was so often drunk in wine and ale for which he had paid. He registered his 'scarlet and white hoop, white cap' racing colours and sent horses to be trained at Danebury by John Day. In 1864 he won the Cambridgeshire with Ackworth, taking nearly £100 000 out of the Ring who knew in their wisdom that such a success would whet the appetite of the rash impetuous milord to such an extent that his eventual downfall was a certainty upon which they could rely.

Meanwhile Hastings had been the central

Harry Hastings, 'the perfect Cocker'. (The Mansell Collection Ltd)

character in a *cause célèbre* which had rocked society when he eloped with Lady Florence Paget, the fiancée of Henry Chaplin, a rich Lincolnshire landowner who was a personal friend and contemporary of the Prince of Wales. No one could defend the dashing and debonair Hastings for this inexcusable action which did not have a redeeming feature, unless it was the saving of Chaplin from becoming married to a young woman who did not love him. The fact that Hastings and Chaplin were friends who moved in the same circle of society added colour and piquancy to an affair which left Chaplin humiliated and stunned.

Even as the *cause célèbre* was being endlessly discussed, Hastings was planning to win the 1865 Derby with The Duke who was installed winter favourite for 'The Blue Riband'. He was aggrieved that society did not see the elopement in the same light as the lower classes who with bawdy vulgarity sniggered over the fact that 'The Markis—Gawd bless 'im' had snatched the betrothed of another, but even more aggrieved that Chaplin did not appear either jealous or revengeful. When, therefore, Chaplin began buying expensive yearlings on a prodigious scale, the unbalanced Hastings determined to purchase on an even larger scale in his efforts to thwart and assert his superiority over 'the Squire of Blankney'.

Consequently, when Chaplin paid William I'Anson the enormous sum of £11 500 for Breadalbane and Broomielaw, ostensibly to win the 1865 Derby, and The Duke upon whom Hastings had pinned his Epsom hopes was scratched, Hastings paid the money-lender Henry Padwick £12 000 for Kangaroo. It appealed to his vanity that he had paid so great a sum for one horse while Chaplin, to whom he felt nothing but animosity, had paid £11 500 for two colts. Neither Breadalbane nor Kangaroo excelled at Epsom behind Gladiateur, but it was evident to society that Hastings, whose marriage was already known to be a failure, would leave no stone unturned in his misguided efforts always to get the better of Chaplin. His judgement was clouded, his heart filled with resentment for Chaplin's self-assurance, and his mind oblivious to the fact that his own ruin was only a matter of time. Two years later the first of the two events so ruinous to Hastings occurred when Hermit, owned by Henry Chaplin, won the Derby. Chaplin had bought Hermit from Mr Blenkiron's Middle Park Stud at Eltham in Kent, on a sunny June afternoon when the famous breeder had held a yearling sale. Hastings was present, and was unperturbed when the slightly small but compact chestnut colt was knocked down to his arch-rival for 1000 gns, even though, ironically, he was the underbidder. The next lot sold was Marksman, destined to finish

second to Hermit in the 1867 Derby. Hermit won four races as a two-year-old, including a biennial at Ascot, and although not a runner for the 1867 Two Thousand Guineas, was greatly fancied for the Derby. A week before the Epsom race his chance went from distinct to forlorn when he burst a blood-vessel in a training gallop at Newmarket. The stable jockey, H. Custance, was released to accept another Derby mount, and Chaplin decided to scratch Hermit forthwith. However, his racing manager, Captain Machell, had other ideas on this subject for he had backed Hermit to win a fortune, refused to give up all hope, and persuaded Chaplin to wait and see if Hermit's trainer, Bloss, could work a miracle.

News of Hermit's misfortune quickly reached the ears of Hastings who stood to lose an immense amount of money if Chaplin's colt won at Epsom. Out of sheer spite he had accepted enormous wagers on Hermit, and now seemed on the brink of winning each and every one of them. That his cup of happiness did not brim over, was due to Bloss and Machell who somehow patched up Hermit and took him to Epsom. The problem was to find a jockey, and at the eleventh hour the unfashionable but competent 21-year-old Johnny Daley was engaged—the terms being £100 for the ride, £100 if he was placed, and £3000 if he triumphed.

The weather on Derby Day was the coldest in memory, with snow and sleet falling as the few spectators who had braved the elements huddled on the Downs where there was little shelter from the bitter wind. The canvas roof of Barnard's stand had been torn to shreds, and the Derby contestants looked miserable as they paraded in front of the grandstand where Henry Chaplin was accompanying the Prince of Wales. Hermit stood shivering in the rain as his huge waterproof rug was taken off but had apparently shrugged off the effects of his burst blood-vessel for although dejected, he looked in magnificent trim. Curiously Chaplin who owned Hermit was a tall man, as was Machell who managed the horse, Bloss who trained him, and Daley who rode him. As Chaplin returned from the paddock to the royal box he met Hastings and told him that he thought Hermit still had a chance and suggested that Hastings could back the colt at long odds to cover the £20 000 that he would owe him if Hermit won. Hastings politely scorned the offer.

After ten false starts Mr McGeorge managed to send the 30 runners on their way. A furlong from home it seemed that Marksman, ridden by George Fordham, was assured of victory, but Hermit was making rapid headway, caught the leader yards from the post and won by a neck with the favourite Vauban a bad third.

Chaplin at 25 won £120 000 on the race, of which a sixth was owed to him by Hastings who had the temerity to ask him for time to pay. Chaplin complied to the request with the utmost good grace, but nevertheless Hastings was sorely tested to find the necessary money to settle his immense debts at Tattersalls the following Monday. That he did so was only due to Padwick who charged him an extortionate rate of interest in return for his financial aid. It seemed that Hasting's ruin was imminent, and that only his superb two-year-old Lady Elizabeth could save him. Already her name was being whispered as the Derby winner of 1868, and she was being acclaimed at Danebury as another Blink Bonny.

At Ascot, 10 days later, Lady Elizabeth spread-eagled her field in the New Stakes, and enabled the incorrigible Hastings to recoup much of his Epsom losses. Always fearless, either through courage or foolhardiness, he risked immense sums on his heroine every time she ran throughout the season. She was victorious on twelve occasions, but her defeat in the Middle Park Stakes left her owner in appalling financial trouble. By the end of the year his Scottish estates were sold, he had resigned from the Jockey Club, and his Donington estate heavily mortgaged. Every available liquid asset had been sold, including his hunters and his racehorses with the exception of The Earl and his beloved Lady Elizabeth.

Throughout the winter Hastings, now sick in mind and body, bolstered up his hopes by persuading himself that either The Earl or Lady Elizabeth would win the Derby. But the Fates had decreed that his final ruin was imminent. His peerless filly had been too harshly treated during her first season, had wintered badly, had become jaded and bad-tempered, and was worn out by her exertions long before Derby Day, even though John Day continued to deceive Hastings as to the true state of her health and ability. 'If' is a small word of huge consequence, but although Lady Elizabeth had little chance of Epsom immortality, Hastings might have won the Derby with The Earl 'if' the colt

had been allowed to run. This opportunity was denied to him because of a very dubious alliance between Day, the bookmakers and the money-lenders who had a lien on the colt and deliberately scratched him at Weatherbys on the eve of the race.

Yet for Hastings there still remained his heroine, and he continued to back her as though settling day did not exist. He walked to the paddock to see her saddled for the Derby as though without a care in the world. The blazing sun of late May was in direct contrast to the snow and sleet of the previous year, and there were those present who wondered if on so glorious a summer's day the Fates might relent and allow Hastings to win back his losses in one enormous final plunge on Lady Elizabeth. There was no relenting, and Lady Elizabeth trailed in ignominiously a long way behind Blue Gown, owned by Sir Joseph Hawley and trained at Kingsclere by John Porter. The filly was an equally dismal failure in the Oaks 2 days later, and Hastings was totally destroyed. If anything at all can be said in his defence it is that, even in defeat, he was a fine loser. He congratulated the winning owners without a qualm, a smile upon his lips even though he knew he had dissipated his entire inheritance.

Hastings, in an effort to forget, cruised upon his yacht in Norwegian waters throughout the summer, thus being spared involvement in the storm caused by Admiral Rous writing a broadside to *The Times* suggesting that Hastings had been shabbily treated by Day and the bookmakers over the scratching of The Earl. His views were amply substantiated after The Earl had won the Grand Prix de Paris and three races at Royal Ascot, and it seemed that 'if' The Earl had been allowed to run at Epsom he would have enabled Hastings to make a fresh start. Desperately ill and impoverished the Marquess returned from his cruise in early autumn and travelled back to Donington where he died in November. His final whispered words were: 'Hermit's Derby broke my heart. But I did not show it, did I?'

The disqualification of Craganour 1913

The 1913 Derby must be considered the most sensational and dramatic one of the 20th century, even discounting the tragedy of suffragette Miss Emily Davison being killed after bringing down King George V's colt Anmer at Tattenham Corner. Craganour, the favourite, passed the winning-post ahead of his rivals, and then suffered the indignity of disqualification in circumstances which for ever will smack of personal animosity, bringing forth the comment from an unbiased quarter that it was 'a travesty of a contest the chief purpose of which is supposed to be that of testing the merits of the leading three-year-olds'.

However, it is necessary as the King in *Alice's Adventures in Wonderland* insisted to 'Begin at the beginning and go on till you come to the end . . .'. Firstly, therefore, the background of Craganour's owner must be appreciated. Mr C. Bowyer Ismay, 39 years old, was the younger son of Thomas Ismay who had started his business career as a shipbuilder in the small thriving Cumberland town of Maryport at the mouth of the River Ellen. Ambitious and enterprising he founded a shipbroking business in Liverpool, acquired the goodwill of a bankrupt shipping company whose house flag of 'white star on a red burgee' he accepted as his own, and eventually established the 'White Star' shipping line with their famous transatlantic liners built by Harland and Wolff. Thomas Ismay died in November 1899, and it has always been assumed that it was at his funeral on a bitterly cold day that one of the mourners, the 1st Duke of Westminster, caught a chill which proved fatal. Thomas Ismay was succeeded as Chairman of the White Star Line by his eldest son, Mr Bruce Ismay, with Bowyer Ismay taking little interest in the day-to-day

running of the business. He preferred to shoot big game in East Africa, and had first registered his colours of 'Neapolitan violet and primrose hoops, violet cap' in 1898. Every season he rented a grouse moor in Scotland, and as one of the hills on the moor at Dalnaspidal was called Craganour, he elected to name the yearling that he bought in 1911 after the hill.

Craganour was sired by Desmond out of the mare Veneration, a half-sister to Pretty Polly. Veneration had been bred in 1900 by Major Eustace Loder at his Eyrefield Lodge Stud on the edge of the Curragh, and 10 years later sold with her foal by Desmond to the famous Sledmere Stud in Yorkshire. The yearling was bought for 3200 gns at the 1911 Doncaster Sales by Bowyer Ismay who sent the colt, who had fetched the highest price of the week, to be trained by 'Jack' Robinson at Foxhill.

Craganour made his début in the New Stakes at Royal Ascot in June 1912, winning with convincing ease, but his victory brought little pleasure to his owner, still stunned by the loss of the ill-fated White Star liner *Titanic* on her maiden voyage across the Atlantic 2 months earlier. His brother and American-born Mrs Bruce Ismay were aboard the *Titanic*, together with a manservant. The manservant drowned when the *Titanic* sank, but both Mr and Mrs Bruce Ismay reached New York in safety. On his arrival in New York Bruce Ismay was branded in several newspapers as a coward, and once the protracted official inquiries in New York and Liverpool were concluded he retired to his estate on the west coast of Ireland, with a stigma attached to his name which was never to be eradicated. Inevitably such a stigma affected other members of the family, who at times were unfairly

THE DERBY 1913.

and unjustly abused.

Meanwhile, Craganour proved himself the best two-year-old in England, ending a brilliant season with victories in the Champagne Stakes at Doncaster and the Middle Park Stakes at Newmarket. In all his races he was ridden by Billy Saxby whose father had been a sergeant-major in the 12th Lancers when they were serving in India. Major Eustace Loder had thought highly of Sergeant-Major Saxby and had been responsible for young Saxby being apprenticed to Sam Pickering's stable and subsequently riding some of the Eyrefield Lodge horses.

As a three-year-old Craganour, despite an initial defeat at Liverpool, started favourite for the Two Thousand Guineas. He made all the running on the stand side of the course, but to everyone's amazement the judge awarded the race to Louvois who raced on the far side of the track some 80 yd wide of Craganour. The majority of spectators thought that Craganour had won by at least a length and the judge's decision was hotly disputed even though the stewards, headed by Major Eustace Loder, took no action. However, both Bowyer Ismay and Robinson vehemently criticised Saxby for riding an indifferent race and for being overconfident. Such criticism infuriated the jockey whose indignation knew no bounds when he was replaced by Danny Maher who easily won the Newmarket Stakes a fortnight later on Craganour—with Louvois only managing to finish third. Maher told Ismay that Craganour was certain to win the Derby, but added that he would not be

The finish of the 1913 Derby. 1 Nimbus, 2 Great Sport, 3 Craganour, 4 Aboyeur, 5 Sun Yat, 6 Aldegond, 7 Bachelor's Wedding, 8 Louvois, 9 Shogun, 10 Prue, 11 Day Comet. (*Illustrated London News*)

able to accept the mount if it was offered to him as he had a retainer from Lord Rosebery and the noble Earl had a Derby runner. This runner was the filly Prue who was not considered to have any chance of success, and Lord Rosebery explained to Maher that he was perfectly willing to release him. Maher, unlike some of the leading jockeys in future years, steadfastly refused the offer, stating that he had a retainer from Lord Rosebery and would honour it. Consequently Ismay decided to bring Johnny Reiff from France to ride Craganour at Epsom while Saxby, furious and smarting with injured innocence, agreed to ride Louvois and other English jockeys took umbrage that an American living in Paris should have been given the mount on Craganour.

Despite the unfortunate outcome of the Two Thousand Guineas Craganour seemed virtually a certainty for the Derby, and he started a short-priced favourite at 6–4. Once the tapes went up

As the runners round Tattenham Corner, Anmer is brought to the ground. (*Illustrated London News*)

Aldegond led, but was soon passed by the 100–1 outsider Aboyeur, followed by Craganour, Nimbus, Sun Yat, Louvois and Shogun. They came down Tattenham Corner in this order, but as they entered the straight the misguided suffragette Emily Davison dashed on to the course bringing down Anmer. This mêlée did not affect the leaders and 3 furlongs from home Craganour drew alongside Aboyeur. No one will ever know exactly what occurred at this precise moment, but certainly both Craganour and Aboyeur came exceedingly close to each other. As they did so Frank Wootton on Shogun attempted to come through on the far rails. One moment there was plenty of room for him to do so, the next the space was totally blocked by Aboyeur and Craganour, whose jockeys were busily engaged in a ding-dong barging match. As this happened, the horses swerved from the rails back to the middle of the course, apparently interfering with Great Sport and Nimbus who were making ground on the outside, while Louvois came between them and the far rails, passing Day Comet and Shogun. It was patently obvious to those in the grandstand that there had been an immense amount of bumping and boring, but as the judge had Craganour's number hoisted into the frame as the winner, the majority of backers heaved a sigh of relief that the favourite had won. Second place was awarded to Aboyeur, third to Louvois and fourth to Great Sport, with the distances a head and a neck. The only criticism of the result was that many believed that the judge had completely missed Day Comet who had clearly finished third. Mr C. Bowyer Ismay

Anmer, the King's horse under which Emily Davison threw herself and died from her injuries. (Radio Times Hulton Picture Library)

led his hero into the winner's enclosure, receiving congratulations on his triumph. Reiff disappeared into the weighing-room followed by Aboyeur's jockey, E. Piper. A few moments later the cry 'All right' was distinctly heard, and a hot jubilant Robinson exclaimed: 'Thank God, I was beginning to get worried.' As he did so, and began instructing a stable-lad to take Craganour away, an official came bursting out of the weighing-room shouting

'Come back!' followed by a serious-faced Lord Durham who stated that the stewards were holding an inquiry and that there was an objection to the winner. Robinson and Ismay, incredulous and grim of countenance, were not the only ones who were dumbfounded. An objection to a Derby winner other than Running Rein was unprecedented. Rumours spread thick and fast as to the outcome, but one fact constantly repeated was that Aboyeur's unfashionable jockey was frightened that he would be reprimanded for not keeping a straight course. Another was that Aboyeur's owner Mr A P Cunliffe, one of the principal patrons of the Druid's Lodge Stable and perhaps the shrewdest gambler in the kingdom, did not intend to object for he saw no reason to do so. Thus it became evident that the objection, lodged by the stewards who became prosecutors and judges, was bound to be upheld. And so it was, with the official verdict being that Craganour was disqualified and placed last on the grounds that he jostled the second horse. The stewards added that Craganour, by not keeping a straight course, had at one point of the race seriously interfered with Shogun, Day Comet and Aboyeur, and had afterwards bumped and bored Aboyeur so as to prevent his winning.

When the news of the disqualification was announced C. Bowyer Ismay, even though mortified and bitterly offended, had the sportsmanship to grasp his trainer by the hand and say: 'Never mind, Robinson. We shall win the Derby again some day.' Robinson was too heartbroken to reply. Three days later, and thus 24 hours too late, Ismay sent to the clerk of the course a notice of appeal against the steward's decision. A fortnight later he attempted to obtain an injunction restraining the stake-holders from paying the winning stakes to Aboyeur's owner, but although an interim injunction was granted, Mr Ismay instructed his solicitors to proceed no further, for by this time he had decided to sell Craganour.

Yet Craganour's disqualification has never totally been explained to the satisfaction of everyone, and certain thoughts, ideas and suspicions have coloured the drama of the 1913 Derby ever since the race was run.

The three stewards of the meeting were Lord Rosebery, Major Eustace Loder and Lord Wolverton. Lord Rosebery, since he had a Derby runner, did not officiate at the inquiry, although he was present when the evidence was heard. For some time it had been thought that there was a vendetta between Loder and Ismay, due in part to Loder's annoyance at Ismay's treatment of Saxby and in part, according to rumour, to a personal feud between them. This should not, however, have clouded Loder's judgement or biased his opinion, and at a later date he stated: 'If I am entrusted with the difficult task of administering the Rules of Racing, I shall apply them without fear or favour, whether the race is the Derby or a paltry selling race.' Added to this is the fact that Loder bred Craganour's dam. What man could have enjoyed disqualifying a Derby winner with whom he was so closely associated. Equally, however, the tragic fact cannot be overlooked that Loder was suffering from Bright's disease, and he was to die from it in July 1914. Medically the disease could cause acute physical discomfort and irrational thought through the nervous system being impaired.

It would be unjust to accuse Loder of being anything other than impartial, but a further thought must be that he had known many drowned when the *Titanic* sank and felt aggrieved against the Ismay family. An unusual fact is that there was never any official criticism of Reiff; no fine for injudicious, careless or even dangerous riding brought against him. The truth will never be known, although certain facts should be mentioned. Craganour was sold to Señor Martinez de Hoz of the Chapadmalal Stud in Argentina for £30 000 within weeks of the Derby, with the stipulation that he never raced again. Aboyeur was sold to Russia for £13 000. Robinson died of angina in 1918, having never recovered from his misery at the disqualification of Craganour. Mr C. Bowyer Ismay died at his home Nazelbeech Hall, Northamptonshire in 1924.

The
heroic invalid-
Humorist 1921

Humorist's victory in the 1921 Derby was gained by a colt whose courage knew no bounds, and who was dead a fortnight after his glorious Epsom triumph. His dramatic and tragic death, caused by a tubercular lung condition, had not been detected when he contested the Derby, and in the circumstances his heroic gallantry was nothing short of miraculous. His millionaire owner, Mr J B Joel, whose meteoric rise to vast affluence had been acquired by business acumen and a total mastery of the South African diamond industry, had seen his 'black, scarlet cap' carried for the first time in 1900. The following year he invited Charles Morton to become his private trainer. The choice proved inspired, for in 1903 Morton sent out Our Lassie to win the Oaks for his new patron. Next came the handicapper Dean Swift who ran in eight consecutive City and Suburbans at Epsom, winning twice and being placed on four other occasions. Following the popular successes of Dean Swift came those of Jest who won both the 1913 One Thousand Guineas and the Oaks. At stud she was barren for her first three seasons and in the fourth produced a dead foal. After these calamities she produced the colt, sired by Joel's stallion Polymelus, to whom the name 'Humorist' was given.

Although Humorist made a winning début in the valuable Woodcote Stakes at the 1920 Derby meeting at Epsom, he had greatly perturbed his trainer a few days earlier when he went off his feed and his coat lost its usual sheen. He missed his Royal Ascot engagements as he was coughing, and next ran in the Champagne Stakes at Doncaster. Although considered a 'certainty' he was defeated by Lemonora, but redeemed his high reputation by winning two of his final three races in the autumn,

and in the third, the Middle Park Stakes, only being beaten a neck.

Humorist wintered well and was fully expected to win the Two Thousand Guineas. Ridden by Steve Donoghue he looked an assured winner a furlong out, but suddenly faltered and was relegated to third place behind Craig-an-Eran and Lemonora.

During the intervening month before the Derby Humorist caused constant worry to Morton, One day he looked a picture of health, the next listless and off his food. Such a rapid change in Humorist's condition bewildered his trainer who knew that Mr Joel's colt, at his best, was a champion. Morton also knew that behind the scenes there were problems as to who would ride Humorist at Epsom. Donoghue, who had ridden the colt in a breath-taking trial gallop before the Two Thousand Guineas, believed that Humorist was virtually unbeatable, had been dumbfounded by his failure at Newmarket yet wanted to ride him at Epsom. However, Lord Derby had first claim on his services and expected to run Glorioso. Donoghue, in whose vocabulary there did not seem to be such words as 'loyalty' and 'honouring a retainer', wriggled, writhed and twisted in his efforts to be released, and eventually succeeded, much to Lord Derby's displeasure.

The crowds at Epsom on Derby Day were immense, despite a coal strike which resulted in there being no excursion trains to the course. Above the cavalcade of cars, buses, charabancs and every conceivable type of carriage and cart which wended its way to Epsom Downs from the four quarters of the compass the airship *R33* sent messages detailing the traffic queues. Aboard the airship was an Automobile Association official who was in wireless communication with the grandstand where a

Steve Donoghue on Mr J B Joel's gallant colt Humorist after winning the 1921 Derby. (London News Agency)

colleague was also in touch with the police, giving them information about the congestion on the roads.

In his grandstand box Mr Joel, superstitiously wearing the same black morning coat, waistcoat and red and black striped tie that he had worn when Sunstar won the Derby in 1911, was entertaining guests who included his brother 'Solly' who had arrived from South Africa especially to see Humorist run. Lord Derby's box adjoined that of Mr Joel, and seeing Morton he beckoned to the trainer and told him categorically that he was waiving his claims to Donoghue for the first and last time while he had a retainer on the jockey's services.

The race needs little description, for Humorist came down Tattenham Corner with Donoghue's boots almost over the rails, was driven into the lead and held on gallantly to withstand the persistent challenge of Craig-an-Eran by a neck with Lemonora three lengths away third. Joe Childs, who rode Lemonora, always insisted that he was an unlucky loser, giving as his reason the fact that as Tattenham Corner was approached Steve called out to Jellis, who was ahead of him on Brinklow, to allow him room to come through on the rails. Jellis complied, but as Childs attempted to follow Steve, Jellis returned to his original position on the rails, thus bringing Lemonora to a standstill. It was a legitimate manœuvre but one which did nothing to harmonise the relationship between Childs on the one side and Donoghue and Jellis on the other.

As Mr Joel proudly led Humourist into the winner's enclosure he was warmly congratulated, and it was pointed out to him that he, Lord Rosebery and the Duke of Portland were the only three men alive to have owned two Derby winners.

Humorist was utterly exhausted after his Epsom triumph, but it was decided to run him in the Hardwicke Stakes at Royal Ascot. Morton sent him to the Ascot stables on the eve of the meeting, but at exercise on Tuesday morning, the Derby winner pulled up after a short gallop with blood pouring from his nostrils. A veterinary surgeon examined him and advised that Humorist should immediately return to Morton's stables at Letcombe Regis for a prolonged rest.

A week later Alfred Munnings, commissioned to paint Humorist, went to stay with the trainer. By lunch-time on the Sunday he had completed his preliminary sketches and told Morton that another hour's work in the afternoon was all that was needed to complete his task. The two men drank a bottle of champagne, lunched and Munnings went into the garden for a siesta. His dreams were shattered when he awoke to hear the trainer's wife crying: 'Wake up, Mr Munnings, Humorist is dead.' Scarcely believing his ears Munnings hastened to the stable yard where he found a distraught Morton in Humorist's box. There was no need for explanations, for the straw was smothered in blood, and pools of it were seeping into the yard under the prostrate body of Humorist. Morton, heartbroken, telephoned Childwickbury and gave the appalling news to Mr Joel, who immediately motored to Letcombe Regis. The body of Humorist was taken to Childwickbury where a veterinary surgeon performed an autopsy which showed that the horse suffered from consumption and severe haemorrhage of the lungs. In the light of the autopsy report Humorist must be acclaimed as one of the bravest of Derby winners, and one of the most tragic in the history of the race.

The triumph
of Windsor Lad
1934

One of the most controversial Derby results occurred in 1934 when HH Maharajah of Rajpipla's Windsor Lad won by a length from Easton, with Colombo, a neck away third. Colombo started at 11–8 against and for all time arguments will rage as to the reasons for his defeat.

Colombo, sired by Derby winner Manna, was undoubtedly the best two-year-old of his generation, and in 1933 was unbeaten in his seven races. Owned by Lord Glanely his victories included the Scarborough Sweepstakes at York, the New Stakes at Royal Ascot, the National Breeders Produce Stakes at Sandown Park, the Richmond Stakes at Goodwood and finally the Imperial Produce Stakes at Kempton Park. Except on his début he was invariably ridden either by Gordon Richards or by Steve Donoghue, who had the mount when he won his final race at Kempton by a short head from Valerius to whom he was conceding 17 lb. As Steve returned to the unsaddling enclosure he was in a high state of glee, for he knew that Gordon Richards's retainer from Fred Darling would prevent his riding Colombo in the 1934 Classics. Steve went further, and admitting to himself that he had been 'in the doldrums' for several seasons, saw in Colombo the means to reassert his mastery by winning the Triple Crown upon Lord Glanely's brilliant colt.

Unbeknown to Steve, however, Lord Glanely was far from happy with his riding of Colombo at Kempton. The owner thought that Colombo should have won by the proverbial street, and was not amused that Donoghue had cheekily won by a short head without recourse to the whip. Such lack of amusement on Lord Glanely's part made him think back to 1919 when racecourse gossip implied

that he was about to offer Donoghue a stupendous retainer. That the retainer never materialised was due to dissatisfaction with Donoghue's riding of Dominion in the Middle Park Stakes, the jockey's refusal to ride He in Lord Glanely's colours in the Cesarewitch, and the final straw when he was beaten on the two-year-old Grand Parade in the Moulton Stakes. This caused a rift between the owner and the jockey which left a permanent scar and which made Lord Glanely wonder if Donoghue's short-head victory on his favourite Colombo was tantamount to an act of deliberate but unsuccessful sabotage.

At the end of the 1933 flat race season Steve Donoghue sailed from Southampton for a holiday in South America. He did not know his exact itinerary and thoughtlessly left no forwarding address. It was an act of folly which was to cost him dear, for Lord Glanely failed in his attempt to contact him regarding the possibility of his riding Colombo in the 1934 Classics. On his return to England Steve was furious to learn that in his absence Lord Glanely had engaged Australian jockey Rae Johnstone to ride Colombo.

Johnstone did not have good fortune in the first few weeks of the 1934 season, and rode 28 consecutive losers before riding his first winner in England. He rented a flat in St John's Wood and spent many evenings with the effervescent Steve who still lived at his flat at the Albany. Outwardly the two jockeys, the veteran and his protégé, appeared the best of friends, but many of Steve's acquaintances believed that beneath the surface he was fuming with rage and indignation. Colombo, ridden by Johnstone, commenced the new season by an effortless victory in the Craven Stakes and an equally convincing triumph in the Two Thousand

Jockeying for position at the mile post. Medieval Knight (Steve Donoghue) leads from
Bondsman (J. Childs) and Windsor Lad (C. Smirke) with Colombo (W. Johnstone) tracking
the leader on the rails. (Radio Times Hulton Picture Library)

Guineas. It seemed that he was invincible.

As Derby Day drew near, punters attempted to
find alternatives to Colombo, but their task was not
easy, for Colombo towered like a colossus above his
contemporaries. Umidwar, Easton and Windsor
Lad appeared his only logical rivals and of these
three Windsor Lad had the best credentials, for he
had won the Chester Vase with an authority which
stamped him as a very good colt and had followed
up this success by a length victory in the Newmarket
Stakes. On a less serious and more superstitious
note his claim was strongly advocated by the Epsom
gipsies who remembered that 60 years earlier Gipsy
Lee had prophesied that no horse would win the
Derby during her lifetime whose name began with
the letter 'W'. Her prophecy proved correct, but in
the autumn of 1933 she had died. Windsor Lad was
the only Derby runner whose name began with the
letter 'W'.

On the morning of the Derby, despite support for
Windsor Lad, Colombo was a red-hot favourite—
so short a price that Lord Glanely was perturbed
and unhappy. He desperately wanted to win a
second Derby and believed that Colombo would be
responsible for making his wish come true, but at
the back of his mind were nagging doubts.

Johnstone had very little experience of Epsom and
Steve Donoghue, although now a veteran, had
unsurpassed knowledge of every blade of grass on
the track. Perhaps he should have allowed Donoghue to ride Colombo, despite rumours that the
jockey was financially in deep trouble and would
have ridden Colombo to lose in an effort to clear his
debts. As it was, he was unable to forget Donoghue
for as his chauffeur-driven car travelled to Epsom,
on many hoardings he saw Steve's face on a watch
advertisement with the caption 'Steve Donoghue
says it is the best watch I had' and, underneath,
'This veteran favourite of the Turf knows what
accurate timing means'. Little could the advertisers
know Steve's reputation for unpunctuality.

No two interpretations of the running of the 1934
Derby will ever coincide. Many believe that
Donoghue conned Johnstone, telling him that his
best tactics would be to allow Colombo to follow
Medieval Knight (Steve's mount) round Tattenham
Corner. From the grandstand it seemed as the
straight was reached that Colombo was neatly
pocketed behind Medieval Knight and full of
running. All that was needed was for Steve to give
him the required opening. This, for reasons best
known to himself, Steve refused to do, and as his

The Finish: Windsor Lad winning by a length from Easton, in 2 min 34 s, with the 'unbeatable' Colombo third, a neck behind Easton. (*Illustrated London News*)

mount, like an ebb tide, began to go backwards he took the luckless Colombo with him. Meanwhile Smirke had given Windsor Lad a copy-book trouble-free ride, and he shot his mount into an unassailable lead which he maintained until the post. It was agreed, among the turmoil of post-race recrimination, that Johnstone had ridden a very ill-judged race and Steve, maliciously stirring up trouble remarked: 'If I had ridden Colombo he would have won on the bit by many lengths. Had any other English jockey ridden him who knew the course, he would have won comfortably.'

Trainer Marcus Marsh elaborated on Windsor Lad's triumph years later when he wrote:

It was the long Indian Summer of '32 and the mood around the sales ring was unusually carefree and contented.

By contrast, my own mood was highly pessimistic. The Maharajah of Rajpipla had asked me to buy him a potential classic horse for £1200 ('See, not a penny more,' he'd said) and even in that day and age, this seemed a remarkably small sum for a would-be hero.

Moreover, the first lot of yearlings I'd seen hadn't impressed me at all. Then into the ring came a colt by Blandford, out of Resplendent, who had been second in the Oaks.

Marcus Marsh, trainer of Derby heroes Windsor Lad and Tulyar—and son of Richard Marsh who trained Persimmon, Jeddah, Diamond Jubilee and Minoru. (Radio Times Hulton Picture Library)

He was big and he was backward and I thought he was the most exciting animal I had ever seen. The passing years haven't changed that opinion one iota. We would come to know him as Windsor Lad.

But standing there that day, I could already picture him fully developed as a three-year-old, dominant and majestic. He was everything I had ever looked for in a horse. He was a colt of great bone and substance with a good head and a good eye. You only had to look at that head and that eye to know that this was one who would never be content with anything short of supremacy.

However, it was really the way he moved that excited me so. He was a marvellous walker, all liberty, with the most superb balance, always perfectly poised on whichever leg he happened to be standing. And this is your one true guide. You have seen them in the boxes, looked them all over, but it's when they begin to move around the paddock that you know.

This one was, to me, such a prince among peasants that I couldn't understand why everyone else didn't crowd around him. I was so sure about him. There wasn't a single doubt in my mind.

I bought him for £1300 and could barely believe my good fortune, but there remained just one more battle to be won.

I sent a telegram to the Maharajah, saying, 'Have bought you potential classic horse by Blandford–Resplendent, £1300.'

I received a reply from him saying, 'Too much money, will not buy.'

So I sent a further wire, saying, 'In which case, will take profit.'

His reply this time was very prompt.

'In which case,' it said, 'will keep.'

I went to bed that night, a very contented man. In all my life, I never did a better day's work.

Ridden by Fred Lane, Windsor Lad ran three times as a two-year-old. First time out on 12 July 1933, over 5½ furlongs at Newmarket, he had been unplaced. Three weeks later, in the six-furlong Richmond Stakes at Goodwood, he had finished fourth behind two high-class two-year-olds, Colombo and Medieval Knight.

He then rounded off the season by winning the Criterion Stakes over 6 furlongs at Newmarket by a head from Lord Astor's Bright Bird.

He hadn't been setting the stands on fire, but I was delighted none the less. I had, after all, never looked upon him as a two-year-old. To me, he had always been a potential Derby horse and I had no intention of rushing him.

He continued to develop nicely throughout the winter months, but he was still backward when March came in, and even then I was a little afraid that the Classics might come too soon for him. We decided to miss the Guineas and set our sights on the Derby. 'Come what may,' I told myself, 'he'll certainly be a Leger horse.'

I already knew that stamina would be his strong suit; and speed was my only worry. I wanted to be convinced that he had the brilliant turn of foot that lifts out the great horses from the crowd. So I asked George Duller, famed steeplechase jockey, whether he'd send along a couple of class horses to rattle along with our colt.

His Highness the Maharaja of Rajpipla leading in his horse Windsor Lad after his colt had won the Derby; Charlie Smirke up. (Radio Times Hulton Picture Library)

He sent two four-year-olds . . . Totaig who had won the Hunt Cup as a three-year-old and Statesman who had been third in the Derby. Totaig was to receive 10 lb from Windsor Lad who, in turn, was to receive a similar amount from Statesman.

Charlie Smirke rode Windsor Lad and had him going comfortably throughout the gallop; and he finished upsides Statesman on the bit to delight us all.

I immediately rang the Maharajah and told him that I considered it worthwhile having a bet on the Derby at long odds. I was to put on £250 each way at the best available odds, which were 40–1, as the stable commission.

I was fortunate to gather a first-class team around me. My head man, Harry Coventry, who later held that post with Atty Pesse; and Tom Dowdeswell who looked after Windsor Lad and was later promoted to be my travelling head man, a position he held with me for over 30 years also helping me to prepare my second Derby winner Tulyar. And with Charlie Smirke riding, I had no worries in that department.

I have no hesitation at all in saying that he was the best jockey I have ever known or ever seen. Over the years, I had men such as Steve Donoghue, Joe Childs, Harry Wragg, Sir Gordon Richards and Charlie Elliott riding for me and I admired them all immensely. Yet none of these, in my opinion, had quite the spark, the genius if you like, that Charlie had.

We next decided to run Windsor Lad in the Chester Vase which was not really suited to such a big, backward and long-striding horse. But I felt that it was all good experience and would teach him to be handy and how to negotiate sharp left-hand bends.

He was only set to carry 7 st 12 which was too low for Charlie; so I engaged Freddie Fox, a genuine lightweight.

He won cleverly by half a length from Zelina, Steve Donoghue up, who had previously won the Greenham Stakes at Newbury. More impressive to me was the way he handled the turns, came away up the short straight, and cocked his ears as he passed the post.

Freddie Fox didn't share my optimism.

'He's a nice horse, all right,' he said, 'but at Epsom he'll have no chance with Colombo. He'll never match his speed. Still, he might be a Leger horse.'

A few minutes later, there were other words on the same subject. Charlie had been watching the race with Colombo's partner, the Australian Rae Johnstone, and discussing Windsor Lad.

'He's a bit of a horse, I'll give you that,' said Johnstone, 'I reckon he'll give me a nice lead into the straight at Epsom.'

'He'll lead you all right,' said Charlie, thoroughly roused, '. . . all the way.'

Now that the summer had broken through, Windsor Lad had begun to bloom and yet I still

thought he looked slack. So as Chester had taken nothing out of him, I decided to run him a week later in the Newmarket Stakes over one and a quarter miles. This time the weight was 9 stone and so Charlie was up, making his first public appearance on the colt.

We were opposed by Lord Rosebery's Flamenco, ridden by Harry Wragg, who had finished fourth in the Guineas, three lengths behind Colombo. On this occasion, it was Charlie who rode the Wragg-like race, tracking Flamenco throughout the early stages. Then coming into the Dip, he made his challenge and in three strides the race was won and lost.

Windsor Lad sailed home by a length and from that moment on I never had the slightest doubt that, barring some terrible blunder on our part, he would win the Derby.

Jack Jarvis who had trained Flamenco was so impressed with Windsor Lad's performance that he straightaway backed him for the Derby.

There were now just three weeks left before the big day and he would not race in public again. We had one last speed trial in which, over 3 furlongs, Windsor Lad made a good little sprinter called Paradise Lost look very ordinary indeed.

Charlie stepped down, very jaunty. 'Boys,' he said, spreading his hands wide, 'we're on.'

I won't pretend that I was all that calm in the interlude leading up to the Derby, but Windsor Lad was a great comfort to me. You couldn't ask for a better horse to train. He was patient, gentle, kind, intelligent and yet never finicky or feminine. He was eating up to 22 lb of corn a day which is a vast quantity of food for a horse.

We took him to Epsom on the Monday and gave him a canter round the course on the Tuesday morning, letting him swing round there with a horse of Stanley Wootton's. And then on Wednesday came what was for me the most difficult time of all . . . the moment around nine o'clock in the morning when, with his preparations finished, you can do nothing else but wait for three o'clock to come around.

I just didn't know what to do. I was staying with Nona, my sister, and I wasn't sure whether it was best to go back there or to go for a walk and have a look at some of the cars parked on the Downs. Anyway, I couldn't really force myself to wander far away from the stables that day.

I had a quick peep at him just before the first race and he looked up at me, tranquil as ever, as if to say, 'What's all the fuss about today?'

Charlie and I had been over the race a hundred times or more and there was really nothing left to say. We were both agreed that if Windsor Lad ever got three lengths clear, no horse on earth would catch him.

His flanks were dry to the touch when I patted him and I felt a stab of pride as I watched him, ears pricked, move down in the long parade past the

Charlie Smirke, at the outset of his career, talking with Stanley Wootton, who was subsequently to become one of Epsom's greatest benefactors. Smirke rode four Derby winners: Windsor Lad, Mahmoud, Tulyar and Hard Ridden. (Syndication International Ltd)

stands. He stopped a couple of times to have a look at the crowd somewhat in the manner of a Brown Jack or a latter-day Arkle.

And it was only then when you saw them altogether that you began to realise what a high-class field this was. Colombo was still the favourite at 11–8, but there were others, too, to catch the eye. There was the Aga Khan's Umidwar, ridden by Harry Wragg . . . the Beckhampton duo of Easton with Gordon Richards up and Medieval Knight, partnered by Steve . . . Bondsman* and Tiberius, a stayer.

Windsor Lad had been drawn in the centre and I could have spotted him on a foggy day. He came out of the gate well and Charlie had him up with the leaders within the first 100 yd.

Steve was bobbing along in front on Medieval

* Bondsman, who raced till he was 17 years old, was used as a hack during the Second World War by General Eisenhower.

Knight, tracked by Colombo on the rails, with Easton, Bondsman and Windsor Lad all in a line. It was still that way at the mile post and our big colt was still going beautifully. Then halfway down the hill, Medieval Knight started coming back and Colombo was boxed in.

Suddenly the whole pattern of the race had changed. If all had gone according to plan, we'd intended to make our challenge in the final furlong. But now with Tiberius in the lead and on the outside rounding Tattenham Corner, Charlie saw the opening he wanted, switched Windsor Lad through on the inside and slipped the field.

Within seconds, he was three to four lengths clear and the race won and lost. This was really where that quicksilver mind of Charlie's made him stand out above the crowd.

Easton did get within striking distance in the final furlong, but there was never any danger, never any need to ride him out . . . and he won by a length and a half, easing up.

The emotion I experienced as I saw him cross the line is almost impossible to describe. There was naturally pleasure and excitement tangled up with such a moment, but dominating all else there was this oceanic sense of relief. All the worrying, all the caring, was over. There had been no disasters, no heartbreaks, at least not for us.

The odd thing was that for weeks, if not months, I had been convinced that Windsor Lad would win. Yet now it had actually happened, I couldn't accept it. And it wasn't until I read about it in the papers the following morning that I was really happy and by then, believe me, I was very happy indeed.

In what was for all practical purposes my first season as an independent trainer, I had won racing's premier prize. I was incidentally, at 29, the youngest one to ever do so.

I went up to Charlie in the unsaddling enclosure and congratulated him.

'We were right,' I said.

'We were,' said Charlie.

And somehow that seemed to sum it all up. We had been lone believers for a long, long while.

Taken from Racing with the Gods *by Marcus Marsh, published by Pelham Books, 1968.*

On the night of the Derby the Maharajah gave a celebration party at the Savoy Hotel. A film of the Derby was shown, and an elephant wearing 'Mr Pip's' purple and cream racing colours was paraded round the dance floor. Charlie Smirke, in irrepressible form, left the party early to join the Crazy Gang at the Palladium. Bud Flanagan persuaded the Epsom hero to come on to the stage to receive the acclaim of the audience. As he stood happily basking in the limelight the Crazy Gang cut his braces with a pair of scissors!

SECTION 3

Famous Derby winners

DIOMED (1780)

The first Derby was run on 4 May 1780 over a distance of a mile. (The distance was increased to a mile and a half after 1783.) Because the race was deemed of no particular importance few details have been handed down. It is known, though, that it was the first race on the card and that the programme included a main of cocks between birds owned by the Gentlemen of Middlesex and Surrey and those owned by the Gentlemen of Wiltshire.

The winner of the Derby was Diomed, ridden by Sam Arnull and appropriately owned by Sir Charles Bunbury, the 'Perpetual President' of the Jockey Club and the foremost figure on the Turf at that time. Bred by Mr Richard Vernon at Newmarket, Diomed was a strongly built chestnut by Florizel, one of the best sons of Herod, out of a mare by Spectator. There is little doubt that Diomed was a high-class three-year-old as he was undefeated at that age, winning seven races of a total value of

£5125, the Derby having been worth £1065. At four he won the Fortescue Stakes and the Claret Stakes at Newmarket and received forfeits in a match. He went wrong at five and never ran, but at six he won a King's Plate at Guildford and was second in two other King's Plates. His racing career ended when he broke down in a race at Lewes.

One hears today of Derby winners that can command a five-figure stud fee. The fee of Diomed, firstly at Up Park near Petersfield, and then at his owner's place Great Barton in Suffolk, was 5 gns. It did at one point escalate to 10 gns only to sink back to 2 gns. He was not a success as a sire in this country, the best of his progeny being Grey Diomed, who was exported to Russia where his influence on breeding was considerable; and Young Giantess, dam of that fine mare Eleanor who won the Derby and the Oaks for Bunbury in 1801.

Diomed had attained the ripe age of 21 when his owner, having no further use for him, exported him to Virginia in the summer of 1798, the price being 50 gns. The purchaser was Colonel John Hoomes, who no doubt congratulated himself when he passed the old horse on to Mr Miles Selden for 1000 gns. It can hardly be said that Diomed's future looked bright particularly as the secretary of the owner of the General Stud Book wrote to a breeder in Virginia:

Mr Weatherby recommends you strongly to avoid putting any mares to Diomed; for he has had fine mares to him here, and never produced anything good.

In fact Diomed, against all the odds, proved an outstanding success. He lived till he was 31 and preserved his virility to the end. He founded a dynasty and from the first Derby winner are descended some of the most famous horses in American racing history—among them Lexington. The latter was a brilliant racehorse until failing eyesight compelled his retirement, and he can be regarded as the greatest of all American sires as he headed the list 16 times, 14 times in succession.

When at last Diomed died it was said there was as much grief among horse-loving Virginians as there had been at the passing of George Washington, and that his death was regarded as a national catastrophe. (*Illustration: page 78*)

WEST AUSTRALIAN (1853)

West Australian was the last and the best of the four Derby winners owned by Mr John Bowes, a son of Lord Strathmore who was unable to succeed to the title as he was born 9 years before his parents married. One of the greatest of 19th-century racehorses, West Australian was not only the first winner of the Triple Crown but in addition carried off the Ascot Gold Cup.

Bred by his owner, West Australian was by Melbourne out of Mowerina, by Touchstone. Melbourne also sired Sir Tatton Sykes, a very good horse that won the Two Thousand Guineas and the St Leger and would have won the Derby, too, but for the unfortunate fact that at Epsom his jockey Bill Scott, who also owned him, was hopelessly drunk. Melbourne was also the sire of the famous north-country mare Blink Bonny, who won the Derby and the Oaks in 1857 and was dam of the 1864 Derby winner Blair Athol. Mowerina was a half-sister to Mündig who won the 1835 Derby for Mr Bowes while his owner was still up at Cambridge; and a full sister to Mr Bowes's 1843 Derby winner Cotherstone.

West Australian was trained by Bill Scott's brother John at Malton and displayed high promise from his earliest days. Sam Wheatley, who trained for the Duke of Cleveland, declared he had never seen a finer yearling. He straightaway backed West

Australian for the Derby and never hedged a penny. In fact it was not all plain sailing for West Australian. He was inclined to be heavy-topped and he had a weakness in his feet that was the cause of intermittent lameness. He did not run as a two-year-old until October. In the Criterion Stakes at Newmarket he performed in a somewhat indolent manner and in consequence was beaten half a length by Speed the Plough. It was the only defeat of his career. Later that week he reversed the form with Speed the Plough in the Glasgow Stakes. Two months previously John Scott had tried West Australian very highly with the four-year-old Longbow who had won the Stewards Cup at Goodwood with 9 st 9. Receiving 21 lb, West Australian had disposed of Longbow with ease.

As a three-year-old West Australian stood 15 hands 3 in and was described in not particularly flattering terms as 'a yellowish bay, rather long in the back with a low stealing action'. He was not seen out before the Two Thousand Guineas which he won by half a length from a very good horse, the Duke of Bedford's Sittingbourne. In the Derby, ridden by Frank Butler wearing the jacket and cap worn by Bill Scott on Cotherstone ten years previously, West Australian was a hot favourite in a field of 28 and sporting Yorkshire was on him to a man. Mr Bowes, who was tending to become a recluse, could not be persuaded to make the journey to Epsom to see his horse run. After the Longbow trial the previous year, he had taken the first fast train to London where he backed West Australian for the Derby to win him £30 000.

West Australian duly won but not with the ease anticipated, and he was all out to beat Sittingbourne by a neck with Cineas a head away third. He was the fifth Derby winner trained by John Scott who had no hesitation in declaring him to be the best horse he had ever trained.

By the autumn West Australian had reached his peak and he won the St Leger in a canter. 'I only touched him once with the whip,' said Butler, 'and I was glad to get him stopped.' West Australian concluded his three-year-old campaign with a couple of walk-overs. At four he ran three times, winning a Triennial Stakes at Ascot; the Gold Cup, though only by a head from Kingston; and a Sweepstakes at Goodwood.

Nowadays a Triple Crown winner would probably be worth at least £2 million. Mr Bowes sold West Australian to Lord Londesborough for 5000 gns and Lord Londesborough stood him at Tadcaster at a fee of 30 gns. Some years later Lord Londesborough resold him to the Duc de Morny for 4000 gns, and on that nobleman's death West Australian became the property of the French

Sir Charles Bunbury's Diomed, winner of the inaugural Derby on 4 May 1780, by George
Stubbs. (Fores Gallery, London)

Emperor. Neither in England nor in France was he
a success as a stallion but through Solon, Barcaldine
and through Marco, Hurry On is descended from
him in tail-male. Hurry On sired three Derby
winners: Captain Cuttle, Coronach and Call Boy.

BLINK BONNY (1857)

Blink Bonny must unquestionably be regarded as
one of the outstanding winners of the Derby. Not
only did she win the Oaks as well but she is the only
Derby-winning filly to have bred a Derby winner,
too. Moreover, she won the Derby in what was then
the record time of 2 min 45 s, a time which was in
fact $11\frac{1}{5}$ s slower than that of the grey Mahmoud in
1936.

Bred, owned and trained by Mr William I'Anson,
a Scotsman who had settled down at Malton in

Yorkshire, Blink Bonny was a bay standing 15
hands $2\frac{1}{2}$ in by Melbourne out of Queen Mary, by
Gladiator. I'Anson had evidently been impressed by
the successes of a horse called Braxey and he set
out to acquire Queen Mary. This proved no easy
matter, but he eventually tracked her down to the
wilds of Scotland and was able to purchase her for
£30. Apart from producing Blink Bonny, she was
the grandam of the Derby winner Blair Athol and
the St Leger winner Caller Ou.

I'Anson was a believer in making his horses
'sweat for the brass' and Blink Bonny ran eleven
times at two, winning eight races including the
Gimcrack Stakes at York. He would have accepted
an offer of £3000 for her from Lord Londesborough
if permitted to retain her in his own stable, but
Londesborough declined to agree to that. Subsequent offers of £5000 and £6000 from other
sources were turned down.

'Returning to Weigh', by J F Herring Sen. West Australian (1853) in Mr Bowes's black racing silks. (Fores Gallery, London)

Blink Bonny, 1857, by Harry Hall. (Arthur Ackermann & Son Ltd)

In the late autumn Blink Bonny began to have serious trouble with her teeth, a common weakness with the stock of Melbourne. She suffered a lot of pain, could eat no corn, only green stuff, and her condition rapidly deteriorated. In the New Year she began to recover but she was nothing like at her best when finishing fifth of eight in the One Thousand Guineas. Her Derby price drifted to 1000–30, and in fact it was reckoned improbable that she would run. Certain bookmakers laid her at extravagant odds in the assumption that she was a non-runner. When her number went up on the board there was a rush to hedge, and she started at 20–1.

The race was a dramatic one. Due to indiscipline and disobedience on the part of certain jockeys who were trying to upset the highly strung favourite, Tournament, the start was delayed for an hour. With a furlong to go M.D. looked all over a winner and his backers were shouting him home when he broke down badly and stopped to nothing. Blink Bonny, Black Tommy, Adamas and Strathnaver finished virtually in line and nobody knew which had won until Blink Bonny's number went into the frame. Second was Mr Drinkald's 200–1 outsider Black Tommy who had been saddled by his owner's valet. 'Thank God I've won the Derby', shouted Mr Drinkald, 'and not a soul is on bar myself!' His jubilation, though, was of brief duration.

None the worse for her hard race in the Derby Blink Bonny, again ridden by Charlton, a Yorkshire jockey, was saddled for the Oaks 2 days later and won with ease. She was given a walk-over in a Sweepstakes at Ascot and then won the Bentinck Memorial Stakes at Goodwood and the Lancashire Oaks at Liverpool.

She was a hot favourite for the St Leger but finished a poor fourth behind the One Thousand Guineas winner Imperieuse. There had been some nasty rumours circulating that she was not going to be permitted to win and an angry crowd surrounded I'Anson after the race. It is quite likely that he would have been lynched but for the timely and effective intervention of the famous pugilist, Tom Sayers. The situation was further inflamed when two days later Blink Bonny won the Park Hill Stakes in a faster time than that recorded by Imperieuse in the St Leger.

It seems certain that Charlton pulled Blink Bonny in the St Leger. I'Anson was not in the plot and had backed his filly to win £3000. He had been warned of what was intended but believed, mistakenly, in Charlton's honesty: with dire result. The instigator was the influential Yorkshire bookmaker John Jackson, a man rarely hampered in his operations by the possession of moral scruples. He specialised in the corruption of jockeys. Confident that Charlton would not hesitate to betray I'Anson if offered sufficient money to do so, he had backed Imperieuse heavily and laid Blink Bonny. His confidence was not misplaced.

Blink Bonny was difficult to train at four and only ran once, being pulled up in the Bentinck Memorial Stakes at Goodwood. She died at the age of eight but not before she had bred Blair Athol, 'the bald-faced chestnut', by Stockwell. Blair Athol won the 1864 Derby despite not ever having been on a racecourse before. His price was 14–1 and he was cheered home by the officers of two cavalry regiments who had backed him to win £23 000. He was a great success as a stallion and was four times champion.

As for the gallant Blink Bonny, her skeleton was set up in the museum at York.

GLADIATEUR (1865)

Gladiateur destroyed belief in the invincibility of the English thoroughbred. The so-called 'Avenger of Waterloo' not only won the English Triple Crown but also the Grand Prix de Paris. No other horse has achieved that feat. Moreover, he won the Ascot Gold Cup at four. He well deserved the noble statue of him that stands just inside the main gates of Longchamp.

He was bred and owned by Count Frederick de Lagrange, the only son of one of Napoleon's generals. In 1857 the Count bought the entire stud of M. Alexandre Aumont, one of the pioneers of bloodstock-breeding in France. The Lagrange Stud at Dangu was superbly equipped and organised: some of the horses bred there were trained in France, others in England, over-all control being vested in Tom Jennings of Phantom Cottage, Newmarket.

Sire of Gladiateur was the French Derby winner Monarque, designated as by The Baron or Sting or The Emperor. Miss Gladiator, Gladiateur's dam, was by Gladiator and was too unsound to be trained. Gladiateur, for all his remarkable record, suffered from intermittent lameness and was far from easy to train. When he was a foal his dam trod on him and this left him with a nasty enlargement on his off-fore. His lameness, though, was not due to that, but to navicular disease.

In appearance Gladiateur was a tall, angular bay and anything but handsome. One evening Tom Jennings, who trained him at Newmarket, was showing a party of Frenchmen round his stable. When they came to Gladiateur Jennings announced: 'This is the horse that pulls my cab when I go racing.' 'Mon Dieu, qu'il est laid,' said one of the visitors. When the tour was over the cry went up: 'But Monsieur Jennings, where is the famous Gladiateur?' The party returned to the cab-horse. 'But Monsieur Jennings, you told us this was your cab-horse.' 'Yes,' replied Jennings with the rough, contemptuous humour deemed appropriate in that era when dealing with foreigners,' but I didn't think even you would be such bloody fools as to believe that.'

Gladiateur did not run as a two-year-old until the Newmarket Second October Meeting partly because he was big and backward, partly because he had begun to suffer from periodic lameness. His first race was the Clearwell Stakes which he won by a length. At the same meeting he dead-heated with Longtown in the Prendergast Stakes. Jennings complained he had been indifferently ridden. At the Houghton meeting he was unplaced in the Criterion Stakes. He was starting to cough and ought not to have run. He was not seen out again that season.

During the winter Gladiateur was so lame that Jennings had him blistered on both forelegs. He hardly left his box during the whole of January and for most of February. There was little time left to get him ready for the Two Thousand Guineas and, in fact, he was only half fit when he took the field for that event. Rules were by no means strict in those days: Gladiateur never went into the paddock before the Guineas and was saddled behind the Ditch. Starting at 7–1, he had the hardest race of his career to win by a neck from Archimedes with three others bunched close up behind.

Between the Two Thousand Guineas and the Derby Gladiateur remained sound and it was possible to give him a thorough preparation. He was subjected to one searching trial from which he emerged with flying colours. He went to Epsom carrying the complete confidence of his trainer, especially as the opposition did not appear to be of a particularly formidable character. Favourite at 5–2, he won with ease. The only moment of peril came when his short-sighted rider Harry Grimshaw was taking things easily in tenth place at Tattenham Corner, quite unaware of the long lead being established by Christmas Carol. Fortunately for Grimshaw, and for all concerned with Gladiateur, Jem Goater on Brahma shouted to him to wake up and get a move on. Gladiateur was given a great reception. This did not stop one French newspaper reporting that he had had to be protected by 600 prize-fighters and that there had been a plot to seize Grimshaw and bleed him before the race so that he would be too weak to ride.

Gladiateur then departed for Paris where, in front of a crowd of 150 000 wildly excited spectators, he was a decisive winner of the Grand Prix. Returning to England, he won two races at Goodwood, one being a walk-over. He was lame for much of the time before the St Leger and won that race from Regalia virtually on three legs. Regalia's owner Mr W. Graham, a rather brash individual who had once been a wrestler and had then made a fortune as a distiller, lodged objections to Gladiateur both before and after the race on the grounds that he was a four-year-old. The stewards declined to consider these objections since Gladiateur had been properly registered with the required veterinary certificate.

Two days after the St Leger Gladiateur won the Doncaster Stakes in a canter. He then paid a brief visit to France to win the Prix du Prince Impérial, returning to England to win the Newmarket Derby by forty lengths. Finally he was asked to shoulder 9 st 12 in the Cambridgeshire, an impossible task for a three-year-old. He would very likely have been placed, though, if only Grimshaw had not thought that he was going nicely six lengths behind the leader when in fact the distance was more like 100 yd.

At four Gladiateur was more or less permanently lame. Nevertheless, he won all his six races, these including two walk-overs. In France he won the Prix de l'Impératrice and La Coupe. He then returned to England to win the Gold Cup in remarkable fashion by forty lengths after being 300 yd behind the leader in Swinley Bottom. His last race was the four miles Prix de l'Empereur: ridden by George Pratt, he won in majestic style.

As a sire Gladiateur was a failure both in England and in France, proving unable to transmit to his offspring his speed, his stamina or his unquenchable zest for racing. His owner sold most of his bloodstock at the time of the Franco-Prussian War and Gladiateur was bought for 5800 gns by Mr Blenkiron of the Middle Park Stud, 200 gns less than the sum paid two years later by the Germans for Breadalbane, whom Gladiateur had literally galloped to a standstill in the Gold Cup.

In 1876 Gladiateur died of chronic navicular disease. A few cynics at Newmarket, who had never been able to accept the idea of the best English horses being fairly and squarely beaten by a French one, shook their heads knowingly and declared he had died of old age. (*Illustration: page 82*)

LORD LYON (1866)

Lord Exeter's Stockwell, foaled in 1849, won the Two Thousand Guineas and the St Leger. A superb specimen of the weight-carrying thoroughbred, he was one of the greatest sires ever to stand in this

Gladiateur, 1865, painted by J F Herring Sen. (Radio Times Hulton Picture Library)

country, earning the proud title of 'Emperor of Stallions'. He was seven times champion sire, got three Derby winners, and in 1866 sons of his occupied the first three places in the Derby. He died in 1870 as the result of an accident: while covering a mare, he fell over backwards, broke off part of his tail and the other part penetrated his bowels.

Stockwell's son Lord Lyon, who won the Triple Crown in 1866, was bred by Colonel (later General) Mark Pearson of Oakley Hall, Kettering, and was out of Paradigm, by Paragone out of Ellen Horne, by Redshank. Ellen Horne also bred Rouge Rose, by Doncaster, dam of the 1880 Derby winner Bend Or. In successive years Paradigm bred the Cambridgeshire winner Gardevisure; Lord Lyon; and Lord Lyon's sister Achievement, one of the most beautiful fillies ever seen on the English Turf, winner of many races including the One Thousand Guineas and the St Leger. Paradigm's daughter Chevisaunce was sold to Lord Falmouth for whom she bred Janette, winner of the Oaks and the St Leger and dam of Janissary, who, though almost

useless for racing, sired the 1898 Derby winner Jeddah. The 5th Earl of Rosebery wanted very much to buy Chevisaunce but could not obtain her and had to be content with her half-sister Paraffin who became a foundation mare of his Mentmore Stud.

Lord Lyon was leased by Colonel Pearson to Mr Richard Sutton, second son of Sir Richard Sutton, a famous Master of the Quorn whose hunting was said to have cost him £300 000—quite a large sum of money in those days. Mr Richard Sutton originally served in the Royal Navy and was with Captain (later Admiral) Rous, in HMS *Pique* when she made her celebrated rudderless voyage across the Atlantic. That uncomfortable experience gave Sutton a certain distaste for life on the ocean wave and he transferred his doubtless valuable services to the Life Guards. His military career, though, was not of lengthy duration. A member of the Jockey Club, Sutton liked to bet and won a lot of money when Gardevisure, leased from Colonel Pearson, won the 1866 Cambridgeshire. It was said of him

Lord Lyon, 1866, by Harry Hall. (Fores Gallery, London)

that since he owned all Piccadilly he could well afford to bet as he pleased.

Trained at East Ilsley by James Dover, formerly head-lad to Samuel Lord at Hednesford, Lord Lyon soon showed that he possessed high ability and during the summer he was very well tried against his three-year-old half-sister Gardevisure who won the Cambridgeshire in the autumn. His first race was the Champagne Stakes at Doncaster in which he dead-heated with Redan who was not opposed in the run-off. Later that autumn he won the Troy Stakes and the Criterion Stakes, both at Newmarket.

Lord Lyon wintered well and was a hot favourite for the Two Thousand Guineas. Ridden by a little-known jockey called Thomas, as Custance had been injured in a fall at Epsom, he won by a length from Monarch of the Glen. In the Derby, Custance up, he started at 6–5 on in a field of 25, the first odds-on favourite for 35 years. He duly won but his victory was by no means easily achieved. Lord Ailesbury's Bribery colt, later named Savernake, was a neck in front inside the distance and it was sheer courage

that enabled the favourite to get his head in front close home. His backers were too overwrought to cheer much when his number went into the frame. Mr Sutton had won £50 000.

The race took a lot out of Lord Lyon who was said to look 'as dry as a chip' at Ascot where he failed to give 6 lb to Rustic, who had been third in the Derby, in the Prince of Wales's Stakes. In October Lord Lyon beat Rustic, who had also been bred by Colonel Pearson, by twenty lengths in a £1000-Match at Newmarket. In the St Leger Lord Lyon had another tremendous battle with Saver-nake and once again it was largely his courage that proved the decisive factor in his victory by a matter of inches. Custance, who again rode him, was oddly grudging about Lord Lyon, regarding him as a lucky horse and certainly not a true stayer. In his reminiscences he wrote: 'It is not generally known that Lord Lyon was a very slight whistler and was fired with a flat-iron.'

Horses needed to be tough in those days; there was no question of Classic winners, even Triple

Crown winners, being wrapped in cotton wool and two days after his gruelling battle in the St Leger Lord Lyon lined up for the Doncaster Cup. He failed to stay and was vanquished by Rama. Later that year, in addition to the Match, he won the Select Stakes and the Grand Duke Michael Stakes, both at Newmarket. As a four-year-old he won six races in succession, including the Ascot Biennial and the Stockbridge Cup, but was then beaten by Rama in a Queen's Plate at Lincoln. In all he won 17 of his 21 races and over £26 000. There have been far better Triple Crown winners but none his superior in pluck. He was retired to the Hurstbourne Park Stud in Hampshire at a fee of 30 gns. He was hardly the success his admirers had hoped but he got a good horse in the Grand Prix winner Minting whose ill-luck it was to be foaled the same year as Ormonde. Lord Lyon also sired the 1877 Oaks winner Placida. He died in 1887.

It only remains to add that Lord Lyon's grandam Ellen Horne, a highly influential brood-mare, was originally purchased for 18 gns by Colonel Pearson as a hack for his wife. It was only when she failed in that role that she was sent to the stud.

GALOPIN (1875)

Galopin was not only a great racehorse but a most influential sire, among his offspring being St Simon who was never beaten and became the most successful stallion in the history of thoroughbred-breeding in this country.

Bred by Mr Taylor Sharpe of Baumber Park, Lincolnshire, Galopin was a bay standing 15 hands 3 in by Voltigeur's son Vedette out of Flying Duchess, by The Flying Dutchman. Mr Sharpe had paid 80 gns for Flying Duchess at the dispersal of the Norfolk Stud and when she was 17 he sent her to the Diss Stud to be covered by Vedette. The following year Flying Duchess together with her foal, later named Galopin, was sent to Tattersalls where they were bought by Mr Blenkiron of the Middle Park Stud for 100 gns. In 1873 Galopin came up at the annual sale of the Middle Park yearlings and on the advice of his trainer John Dawson, Prince Batthyány bought him for 520 gns. In later years the allegation was made that Galopin was really by Delight who also stood at the Diss Stud. To support this theory the stud groom at Diss stated that Vedette was paralysed at the time of the visit of Flying Duchess. In any case it was common knowledge that the Diss Stud was run in a deplorably haphazard manner. However, Galopin possessed so many of the traits of the Blacklock family that it is reasonable to assume that Vedette was indeed his sire.

Prince Batthyány was Hungarian by birth. He came to England in his youth and like other Central Europeans of his class he was immediately attracted by the life open to a young man in this country with good looks, sporting tastes and plenty of money. He became a familiar and popular figure on English racecourses and was elected to the Jockey Club in 1859, 16 years after he had started his stud. He spared no expense in the maintenance of his Newmarket establishment, the horses being decked out in scarlet clothing, the lads in blue livery and tall hats. At first he was not very successful in his racing ventures but his luck changed for the better after John Dawson became his trainer. He died of a heart attack on the steps of the Jockey Club luncheon-room in 1884, having become over-excited at the prospect of Galliard, a son of his beloved Galopin, winning the Two Thousand Guineas.

At two Galopin won the Hyde Park Stakes at Epsom on an objection, and then the Fern Hill Stakes and the New Stakes at Ascot. In the Middle Park Stakes he was most unluckily beaten in a close finish by Plebeian and Per Se, having been almost knocked over coming into the Dip. Such was his speed that Dawson was keen to match him against the champion sprinter Prince Charlie but Prince Batthyány was too fond of Galopin to subject him to so severe a test.

Galopin had only one outing before the Derby, a £500-Match over the Rowley Mile at Newmarket against Mr Chaplin's filly Stray Shot whom he beat by ten lengths. Favourite for the Derby at 2–1 and ridden by Morris who was notoriously hard of hearing, he won comfortably by a length from Claremont. At one point Morris was taking matters rather too nonchalantly and it was probably just as well that George Fordham shouted out 'Go on, Deafie!' to warn him that Claremont was getting dangerously close. Years later, penniless and utterly forgotten, Morris died in a cellar.

Galopin displayed his versatility by turning to sprinting at Ascot and making hacks of his opponents in the five furlongs Fern Hill Stakes. He was not engaged in the St Leger but in the autumn, in receipt of 12 lb, he defeated the five-year-old Lowlander in a £1000-Match over the Rowley Mile. Two days later he ran in the Newmarket Derby and had little difficulty in beating Mr W S Crawfurd's Craig Millar who had won the St Leger. That proved to be the final race of his career: there was nothing wrong with him but his owner suffered from a weak heart and the doctors thought that the excitement of watching Galopin run might well bring about the Prince's death.

At the stud Galopin made rather a slow start but in 1883 he was second to Hermit, while he was champion sire in 1888, 1889 and finally, at the great

Galopin, 1875. (*The British Racehorse*)

age of 26, in 1898. The best horse he sired was St Simon. He also sired Donovan, who won the Derby and the St Leger in 1889; Galliard and Disraeli, who both won the Two Thousand Guineas; Galeottia, winner of the One Thousand Guineas and dam of Gay Laura who bred the war-time Triple Crown winner Gay Crusader; and Aida who won the One Thousand Guineas and bred Herself, dam of the Oaks winner Chatelaine. Galopin was 26 years old when his daughter Galicia was born. She bred one of the greatest horses of this century in Bayardo who combined brilliant speed with stamina and whose 22 victories included the St Leger, the Eclipse Stakes and the Gold Cup. Galicia was also dam of the Derby winner Lemberg who won 16 other races including the Coronation Cup, while he dead-heated with Neil Gow in the Eclipse Stakes. Silesia, a daughter of Galicia, bred My

Dear, winner of the Oaks and the Champion Stakes.

After Prince Batthyány's death, Galopin was bought for 8000 gns by Mr Henry Chaplin and stood at the Blankney Stud till his death in 1899. In his old age he got very plump and was said to resemble a shooting cob.

ORMONDE (1886)

Ormonde was one of the greatest horses ever to grace the English Turf. He was never beaten and Fred Archer rated him only a shade inferior to St Simon. Other judges such as John Porter, who of course was biased, and Richard Marsh who certainly was not, placed Ormonde at the top of the tree.

Ormonde was bred at Eaton, in Cheshire, by

Hugh Lupus, 1st Duke of Westminster and was by the Duke's 1880 Derby winner Bend Or out of Lily Agnes, by the 1863 Derby winner Macaroni out of Polly Agnes. As a foal Polly Agnes had been so mean and small that her breeder Sir Tatton Sykes gave her to his stud groom James Snarry on condition he removed her from Sledmere forthwith. Snarry kept Polly Agnes to breed from and in due course she produced Lily Agnes who was nothing much to look at and was touched in her wind but was a stout-hearted stayer that won over 20 races including the Northumberland Plate, the Doncaster Cup and the Ebor Handicap.

In 1880 Lily Agnes was sent to Eaton to be mated with Bend Or's sire Doncaster. The Eaton Stud groom Chapman took a great liking to her and persuaded the Duke of Westminster to buy her for £2500 plus two nominations to Bend Or whose fee was £200. The following season Lily Agnes was mated with Bend Or, the produce being Farewell, winner of the 1885 One Thousand Guineas. She returned to Bend Or the following year and produced Ormonde.

Lily Agnes carried Ormonde a month longer than normal and when born his mane was 3 in long. To begin with he was very much over at the knee and Chapman described him as 'a three cornered beggar that might be anything or nothing'. His appearance soon improved, though, and when he joined Porter's stable at Kingsclere, Porter told the Duke that Ormonde was the best yearling the Duke had ever sent him. Bay in colour, Ormonde stood 16 hands when fully grown. His neck was a trifle short but very powerful, and his head was of exceptional width between the ears. He had excellent bone, a straight hind leg and very strong quarters. His temperament was equable and he was a splendid doer. He was not an attractive mover in his slower paces and a noticeable weakness was his very low withers. Archer always said you felt you were sitting on his neck till he began to gallop. The Duke, an accomplished horseman, once rode Ormonde at Kingsclere and did not much enjoy the experience. Such was Ormonde's power of propulsion that he expected to be pitched out of the saddle at every stride.

During his first winter at Kingsclere Ormonde threw two splints below the knee and as a two-year-old he did no serious work before August. His first race was the Post Sweepstakes at the Newmarket Second October Meeting. He was opposed by a very fast filly called Modwena and beat her by a length with a bit in hand. He had two other races at Newmarket that autumn, the Criterion Stakes and the Dewhurst Stakes, and won them both with ease. He was widely recognised as a likely winner of the Derby.

The following spring there was a strong field for the Two Thousand Guineas. Mat Dawson reckoned that Minting, winner of the Champagne Stakes and the Middle Park Stakes, was unbeatable and Dawson's standards were exceptionally high. There was a lot of support, too, for Archer's mount Saraband. The race proved a duel between Ormonde and Minting who took each other on from the start. Minting became unbalanced coming down to the Dip and Ormonde drew clear up the hill to win by a couple of lengths. Dawson took Minting's defeat very hard. After the race he left the course, retired to his bedroom and stayed there for the rest of the meeting. He was wise enough to realise it was pointless to oppose Ormonde in the Derby and went instead for the Grand Prix de Paris which Minting won.

The Derby was regarded as a match between Ormonde and The Bard who was owned in partnership by General Owen Williams and Robert Peck and who had won all his 16 races at two. The Bard certainly put up a gallant fight but Archer on Ormonde was always holding a doublehandful and Ormonde beat his stout-hearted little rival decisively. At Royal Ascot Ormonde won the St James's Palace Stakes and the Hardwicke Stakes, in the latter event trouncing the 1885 Derby winner Melton. He won the St Leger in a canter and after that three races at Newmarket, the Great Foal Stakes, the Champion Stakes and the Free Handicap. He also received walk-overs in the Newmarket St Leger and a Private Sweepstakes.

It had been a wonderful season for Ormonde but there was a distinctly unpleasant fly in the ointment. Before the St Leger it had been discovered that Ormonde was unsound in his wind. During the winter various remedies were tried, much against the wishes of Porter who, justifiably as things turned out, had absolutely no faith in them. On foggy mornings on Kingsclere Downs it was possible to hear Ormonde half a mile away but astonishing to relate his form remained unaffected. He did not run until Ascot, where he won the Rous Memorial Stakes conceding 25 lb to the three-year-old Kilwarlin who subsequently won the St Leger. His second race at Ascot was the Hardwicke Stakes in which he was opposed by Minting, Mat Dawson being unwilling to believe that his horse could be vanquished by a roarer. After a magnificent race, Ormonde won by a neck. His performance was all the more meritorious as Barrett, who thought he ought to have been given the rides on Ormonde following Archer's lamentable death, deliberately bored Phil in at him and Ormonde had strips of skin torn off his hind leg above the hock.

Ormonde was given a great reception and he and his owner were cheered again and again as the Duke

Ormonde, 1886, by Emil Adam. (The Jockey Club, Newmarket)

proudly led his colt twice round the paddock and almost back to the stables. His final race was the six furlongs Imperial Gold Cup at Newmarket which he won easily from Whitefriar. During the Queen's Golden Jubilee celebrations he was taken up to London where he was the centre of attraction at a big garden party at Grosvenor House. Eastern potentates paid homage to him and fed him on the ducal geraniums and carnations. He appeared to enjoy himself thoroughly.

Ormonde served his first stud season at Eaton and his first crop of foals included good horses like Orme and Goldfinch. For his second season he was leased to Lord Gerard but became ill and got few mares in foal. When he had recovered he was sold by the Duke for export to Argentina for £12 000. He was not a success there, and when transferred to the United States he became a very poor foal-getter. The Duke was sharply criticised for selling a great horse like Ormonde for export; he replied quite reasonably that Ormonde was a roarer himself and had roarers among his ancestors. It was highly

undesirable that he should perpetuate his infirmity in this country.

On his transference from Argentina to America, Ormonde spent a short time in England and Porter went to Netley to see him. It was not a happy reunion as Ormonde, usually so kindly, tried to savage him the instant he entered his box. Ormonde was put down in 1904, his skeleton being returned to England and set up in the Natural History Museum, South Kensington.

ISINGLASS (1893)

Winner of the Triple Crown in 1893, Isinglass was one of the greatest of 19th-century English thoroughbreds. In an era when prize-money was low compared to modern standards he won £57 455, a record amount until surpassed by Tulyar's winnings nearly 60 years later.

Bred and owned by Mr (later Colonel) H. McCalmont, Isinglass was a big, powerful bay by

Isonomy out of Deadlock, by the St Leger winner Wenlock. Isonomy did not run in the Classics, his owner preferring to keep him for a betting *coup* in the Cambridgeshire. He subsequently won two Ascot Gold Cups. There was a frequently told story that Captain James Machell had sold Deadlock since he considered her to be more or less useless, but when her son Gervas started to win races he decided to buy her back again. She proved difficult to locate but, according to this story, Machell eventually discovered her pulling a cart belonging to a farmer who had come to his yard looking for a cart-horse sire.

The facts are more prosaic. Deadlock never ran, and Machell bought her from Lord Alington for 19 gns. Before Gervas had started winning races, Machell had resold her and she had passed through several hands before Machell bought her back. Even then he did not retain her for long, passing her on to McCalmont, in foal to Isonomy, a year later. Two years afterwards she was again covered by Isonomy and produced Isinglass. Harry McCalmont was a thorough sportsman, cheerful and generous. While serving in the Royal Warwickshire Regiment he inherited a fortune from a somewhat eccentric uncle. He forthwith transferred to the Scots Guards and plunged boldly into the racing world, appointing Machell to supervise his interests.

James Machell was one of the most remarkable racing personalities of his era. The son of a parson, he was for a time an impecunious officer, noted chiefly for his prowess in running and jumping, firstly in the unfashionable 14th Foot and then in the equally unfashionable 59th Foot which he left after a row with his Colonel over the question of leave to go racing. Never a popular man, prone to be over-suspicious and in later life subject to melancholia and gout, he had a remarkable flair for the Turf and was an excellent judge of horses, particularly of steeplechasers. He managed to combine in due course, often with considerable success, the different functions of owner–breeder, professional backer, bloodstock agent and racing manager. A lot of rich young men chose to be guided by Machell in their racing ventures and most of them departed a good deal poorer: chiefly, it must be said, because they did not confine themselves, above all in betting, to the advice that Machell provided. McCalmont did not lose his money and was a rich man when he died in the prime of life in 1902. He had been responsible for introducing steeplechasing to Newmarket, laying out the Links course and having the stand constructed.

Isinglass was trained at Newmarket by the former steeplechase jockey James Jewitt whose stable Machell controlled. Handsome and quick-tempered, Jewitt was highly capable and he and Machell were a strong combination though 'they fought bitter and regular like man and wife' and sometimes their disputes resounded from one end of the Heath to the other. At two Isinglass won his first race at Newmarket in the spring and then the New Stakes at Ascot. His only other race that year was the Middle Park Plate which he won from Ravensbury, Le Nicham and Raeburn. The form in the Middle Park worked out well as Isinglass and the other three horses were the only ones to obtain a place in the Two Thousand Guineas, the Derby and the St Leger the following year.

The ground was desperately hard in 1893 and it was very difficult to get a heavy-topped horse like Isinglass fit, particularly as he was indolent by disposition. The state of the going meant that Isinglass was far less impressive in his races than he would doubtless have been under more normal conditions, and usually at one stage the cry went up of 'The favourite's beat' before he eventually scrambled home. Jewitt declared it was quite impossible to get him fit for the Guineas and wanted to strike him out: Machell disagreed and insisted on Isinglass being taken out twice a day and cantered time after time up the tan gallop on Bury Hill. Starting at 5–4 on, Isinglass vindicated Machell's determination to run him by winning the Guineas but he made hard work of his task of beating Ravensbury and Raeburn. Two weeks later he won the mile and a quarter Newmarket Stakes.

In the Derby Isinglass started at 9–4 on. The course at Epsom was harder than a usurer's heart and Isinglass was again a somewhat unimpressive winner. Indeed, at one point, Raeburn looked like beating him, but then Tommy Loates got busy with his whip and Isinglass rallied to win by a length and a half from Ravensbury with Raeburn third. The short-legged Loates was not in the least suited to Isinglass who, in addition to being lazy, was very broad in the back, causing Loates to depend too much on his whip.

Isinglass did not run again before the St Leger which he won by half a length from the unfortunate Ravensbury trained by William Jarvis, father of Sir Jack Jarvis. To add to his bad luck that season, Ravensbury was placed second in the Grand Prix de Paris when everyone bar the judge reckoned he had won. Ten days after the St Leger Isinglass met with the one defeat of his career, being beaten half a length by Raeburn, to whom he was giving 10 lb, in the one mile Great Lancashire Stakes at Manchester. That great mare La Flêche, then a four-year-old and giving Isinglass 6 lb, was third. Raeburn, a half-brother by St Simon to the Derby winner Donovan, was a pretty good horse. Moreover, a mile was really too short for Isinglass who furthermore had had to make his own running which he hated.

At four Isinglass beat Bullingdon and the Derby winner Ladas in the Princess of Wales's Stakes at Newmarket, but the ground was hard and he only scraped home by a head. It rained that night and it rained every day until the Eclipse Stakes a fortnight later. At last Isinglass had the going that suited him, and he showed his appreciation by beating Ladas and his old rival Ravensbury in truly masterful fashion. In the autumn he won the Jockey Club Cup. His one race at five was the Gold Cup which he won without difficulty. He was then retired to his owner's stud at Cheveley, and on Colonel McCalmont's death he, together with all the rest of the Colonel's horses, was taken over by Lord Howard de Walden.

Perhaps because the tail-female line of Deadlock was weak Isinglass hardly did as well as was expected of a stallion. However, his stock won 320 races worth over £166 000 and included Cherry Lass (One Thousand Guineas), Glass Doll (Oaks), John O'Gaunt (second in the Two Thousand Guineas and the Derby, sire of Swynford), Louvois (Two Thousand Guineas), Lady Lightfoot (dam of the St Leger and dual Gold Cup winner Prince Palatine), Cornfield (dam of the Oaks winner Love In Idleness) and Glasalt (dam of the One Thousand Guineas winner Canyon).

Incidentally, Isinglass's sire Isonomy is the only stallion to have sired two Triple Crown winners, the other being Common, not nearly such a good horse as Isinglass. (*Illustration: page 90*)

PERSIMMON (1896)

Foaled in 1893, Persimmon was the last horse to win the Epsom Derby and the Ascot Gold Cup. Ocean Swell won the Gold Cup in 1945, having won the Derby, which was run at Newmarket, the previous year.

Bred and owned by the Prince of Wales, later King Edward VII, Persimmon was by St Simon out of Perdita II by Hampton. Perdita II had been bought for 900 gns on the Prince's behalf by John Porter of Kingsclere who was then his trainer. 'You'll ruin the Prince,' grumbled old Sir Dighton Probyn when he handed over the cheque on the Prince's behalf. In fact Perdita II proved a gold-mine. Two of her offspring, Persimmon and his brother Diamond Jubilee, won the Derby: a third brother, Florizel II, sired the 1901 Derby winner Volodyovski. All told, the sons and daughters of Perdita II won 26 races worth over £72 000, a lot of money for those days when the Derby was worth less than £6000 to the winner.

Trainer of Persimmon was Richard Marsh, once a successful rider over fences. The Prince's horses had left Porter's stable in 1893, the reason given—in fact there were others—being that Newmarket was a lot closer to Sandringham than Kingsclere. From his earliest days Persimmon showed high promise. In appearance he was a lengthy bay with a bold head, slightly lop-ears, perfect shoulder and impressive power behind the saddle. He was inclined to be high-mettled and could be difficult when in the mood, but he fortunately did not possess the dangerously savage temper of Diamond Jubilee. Persimmon's first race, the Coventry Stakes at Royal Ascot, he won impressively. He next won the Richmond Stakes at Goodwood. He scored with ease but Marsh had noted how Persimmon sweated up beforehand and decided that a colt with such high courage and nervous energy would always require careful handling.

Persimmon's only other race that season was the Middle Park Stakes, in which he was a moderate third behind Mr Leopold de Rothschild's St Simon colt St Frusquin and Omladina, a fast filly that had won the Champagne Stakes. In fact Persimmon had been coughing not long before the race: Marsh had not wanted to run him but his wishes were overruled by those of Lord Marcus Beresford, the Prince's racing manager. The race might have done Persimmon a good deal of harm, but Jack Watts had the sense to drop his hands as soon as Persimmon was beaten.

Persimmon was slow to come to hand at three and did not run in the Two Thousand Guineas won by St Frusquin. His first serious Derby gallop proved a total fiasco. 'A nice sort of Derby horse,' observed Lord Marcus Beresford. Another gallop 4 days later was far more satisfactory. The final gallop took place in front of the Prince and Princess of Wales and the Duke and Duchess of York. Persimmon did all that was asked of him most impressively and it was clearly going to take a very good horse to defeat him at Epsom.

It was planned for Persimmon to travel by train from Dullingham Junction to Epsom. Usually a placid and easy-going traveller, he selected this particular occasion for a display of stubborn bloody-mindedness and refused to enter his box. Two special trains left without him and there were only 15 minutes left before the third and final one departed. Marsh, distraught with frustration and worry, then played his last card. He collected a force of twelve lusty volunteers and together they virtually carried Persimmon into his box. Once inside, he settled down quietly to enjoy his feed.

Derby Day was sultry, the course hard and in places rough. Persimmon was sweaty and irritable. Perhaps it was lucky for his supporters that rules

Isinglass, 1893, by Emil Adam. (The Jockey Club, Newmarket)

were still lax in those days and he was not subjected to any long-drawn-out preliminaries. Saddled down in Sherwood's yard, he took no part in the parade or in the canter in front of the stands. St Frusquin, saddled in the grounds of Lord Rosebery's house The Durdans, was a hot favourite at 13–8: Persimmon was a 5–1 chance.

With a quarter of a mile to go the issue lay between those two. St Frusquin was in front on the rails but Persimmon and Jack Watts were steadily reducing the gap. Inside the distance Persimmon suddenly faltered. At this critical juncture Watts, with exemplary coolness, steadied Persimmon, got him perfectly balanced and then drove him home for all he was worth to win an unforgettable race by a neck. It had been a superb piece of riding by Watts.

There followed scenes of the utmost enthusiasm and the whole vast crowd went wild with delight. Only Watts, never a cheerful character when he was having problems with his weight, remained silent and glum. This was too much for the exuberant

Marsh who slapped him on the thigh and shouted: 'Don't you realise you have just won the Derby for the Prince of Wales?' Watts then permitted himself the rare luxury of a faint and transitory smile.

The following month Persimmon and St Frusquin met again in the Princess of Wales's Stakes at Newmarket. They ran wonderfully true to form and St Frusquin, receiving 3 lb, won by half a length. Persimmon did not run in the Eclipse Stakes which provided St Frusquin with a further success. Unfortunately, St Frusquin went wrong before the St Leger which Persimmon won comfortably, starting at 11–2 on. Persimmon concluded his three-year-old campaign by beating the 1895 Derby winner Sir Visto in the Jockey Club Stakes at Newmarket, a race then far more valuable than the Derby or the St Leger.

At four Persimmon had filled out in the right places and was better than ever before. His first race, and his main target, was the Gold Cup. 'When Persimmon was stripped for the Ascot Cup,' recorded that great trainer George Lambton, 'he

Persimmon, 1896, by Emil Adam. (The Jockey Club, Newmarket)

stands out in my memory as the most perfectly trained horse I ever saw, and on that day it would have given my two heroes, St Simon and Ormonde, as much as they could do to beat him.' Persimmon won the Cup by eight lengths from the much-fancied Winkfield's Pride.

Persimmon then reverted from 2½ miles to 1¼ to win the Eclipse Stakes, a double repeated in 1922 by Golden Myth. The summer of 1897 was hot and dry, and those two races on hard ground were more than Persimmon could stand. He threw out two spavins, one on each hock, and was accordingly retired to the stud at a fee of 300 gns. His first crop of runners included the mighty Sceptre who won every Classic bar the Derby. He got Keystone II and Perola who both won the Oaks: Prince Palatine and Your Majesty, winners of the St Leger; and Zinfandel who, like Prince Palatine, won the Gold Cup. Unfortunately, Persimmon broke his pelvis at the comparatively early age of 15 and had to be destroyed. He was four times champion sire and four times leading sire of brood-mares.

GALTEE MORE (1897)

During the latter half of the 19th century there was both expansion and improvement in the Irish bloodstock-breeding industry. A breeder who played a notable part in this was Mr John Gubbins, a great man to hounds and for many years Master of the Limerick. As a young man he had the luck to inherit a large fortune from an uncle and he thereupon established two studs, Bruree and Knockany, in the famous Golden Vale of Limerick. He brought mares with fine pedigrees to fill these studs, and at one point in the 1890s he owned half a dozen stallions

Among Mr Gubbins's mares was Morganette whose price had certainly not been more than £300. Bred in 1884 by Mr J H Houldsworth, she was of no account on the racecourse but had an excellent pedigree being by Springfield out of Lady Morgan, a half-sister of the Oaks and St Leger winner Marie Stuart and a granddaughter of the Oaks winner Miami. Springfield had the speed to win the six furlongs July Cup twice, while in the Champion Stakes he defeated the Derby winner Silvio.

Morganette's third foal was Blairfinde, by Mr Gubbins's own stallion Kendal, by Bend Or, who had won half a dozen races in brilliant style as a two-year-old before breaking down. Trained by Sam Darling at Beckhampton, Blairfinde was sent to the Curragh for the Irish Derby, which he won by twenty lengths. Three years after producing Blairfinde, Morganette foaled a full brother to him named Galtee More after the highest peak in the mountains overlooking the Golden Vale. Galtee More soon showed high promise on joining Darling's stable and his one defeat as a two-year-old was when Glencally beat him by inches in the Lancashire Breeders Stakes at Liverpool. He won the Molecomb Stakes at Goodwood, the Rous Plate at Doncaster and the Middle Park Plate at Newmarket. In the Middle Park he made mince-meat of Lord Rosebery's fast colt Velasquez, winner of the New Stakes at Ascot, the July Stakes at Newmarket, the Prince of Wales's Stakes at Goodwood and the Champagne Stakes at Doncaster.

Bay in colour and of almost faultless conformation, Galtee More was better than ever at three. Ridden by Charles Wood, he was hardly out of a canter to win the Two Thousand Guineas from Velasquez and then, starting at 100–6 on, he completely outclassed the opposition in the mile and a quarter Newmarket Stakes. In the Derby he started at the unrewarding price of 4–1 on, and again partnered by Wood whose licence had only recently been restored by the Jockey Club, he won by a comfortable two lengths from the unfortunate Velasquez. After the memorable victory of the Prince of Wales's Persimmon the year before, the Derby was rather a tame affair but a large contingent of the winner's Irish supporters did their exuberant best to liven things up.

At Ascot, starting at 33–1 on, Galtee More won the Prince of Wales's Stakes. He followed that up by winning the Sandringham Cup at Sandown, the St Leger in which he started at 10–1 on, and the Sandown Park Foal Stakes. An attempt to win the Cambridgeshire with 9 st 6 proved too much for him. His achievements that season had naturally caused the utmost enthusiasm in the land of his birth. He was the very first Irish-bred colt to win the Derby, let alone the Triple Crown, and after his Epsom triumph it was reported that the Galtee Mountains were 'alight with whisky'.

At the end of the year Mr Gubbins sold Galtee More, who had won over £26 000 in stakes, to the Russian Government for £21 000. Some comic stories were soon in circulation about this sale. Apparently the Russian deputation included a certain General Arapoff who claimed to own a vodka distillery. Before arriving at Beckhampton to see Galtee More, he fortified himself with a beaker of neat whisky in the Ailesbury Arms at Marlborough and was so overcome with enthusiasm after seeing Galtee More canter for 3 furlongs that he hurried back to Darling's house, removed a picture of Galtee More from the wall and made off with it.

That evening, Mr Gubbins entertained the Russians at Prince's Restaurant in London, where the General was apparently under the impression that all the ladies dining there had been assembled for his particular gratification. To avoid further embarrassment it became necessary to transfer him to the Empire where no offence was taken when he accosted such ladies as took his fancy. In the meantime Mr Gubbins, who was liable to turn crusty when afflicted by twinges of gout, had got fed up with the whole business and called the deal off. Next morning, however, he was in a better mood and the transaction was duly completed.

Galtee More did well in Russia before being passed on to the Germans for £14 000. He got a lot of good winners in Germany, including Orchidee II, dam of Oleander, one of the best horses ever to race in that country. Previously he had got Irish Lad, rated the best horse ever bred in Russia. He died in 1917.

Eight mares have bred two Derby winners and Morganette is one of them. In 1899 she bred Ard Patrick, by St Florian, who won the Derby in 1902, beating Sceptre. He also won a famous race for the Eclipse Stakes in 1903, when he beat Sceptre and the Triple Crown winner Rock Sand. He was exported to Germany.

FLYING FOX (1899)

The 1st Duke of Westminster is the only man to have owned two winners of the Triple Crown. The first was Ormonde in 1886, the second Flying Fox in 1899, the year of the Duke's death. Had he lived a few years longer the Duke might conceivably have had a third as he was the breeder of that famous race-mare Sceptre. In 1902 Sceptre, despite the way she was exploited by her gambling owner Mr Robert Sievier and the eccentric manner in which she was trained, won every Classic race bar the Derby. It is difficult to put a limit to the heights to which she might have risen had she carried the colours of the Duke and been trained by John Porter.

In 1893 Porter bought a mare called Vampire from Mr Noel Fenwick for the Duke for 1000 gns. She was by Galopin out of Irony, by Roseberry. She

Galtee More, 1897, (*The British Racehorse*)

soon made her presence felt at Eaton by her savage temper and after she had tried to eat a stud hand and had the temerity to attack the Duke himself, the Duke decided to get rid of her. Porter said he was perfectly willing to take her on himself, whereupon the Duke changed his mind and decided to keep her. Her first foal she killed in a temper. However, then came Batt who ran second to the 100–1 outsider Jeddah in the 1898 Derby. After Batt, she produced Flying Fox, a bay colt by Orme. By Ormonde out of a sister to St Simon, Orme was a top-class horse that won five races at two while his successes at three included the Eclipse, Sussex and Champion Stakes. It was the big racing sensation of the 1890s when he was poisoned not long before the Two Thousand Guineas and nearly died. The perpetrator was never discovered, though Porter strongly suspected one of his own employees. Orme was selected as Vampire's mate because he stood at Eaton and it was thought inadvisable to send Vampire away because of her unreliable temper. The disadvantage of this union was that Orme returned to her the hot Galopin

blood with only one free generation. It would have been surprising if Flying Fox had turned out to be a thoroughly placid individual.

Spare and wiry and with a beautiful action, Flying Fox in training soon showed Porter his ability and just occasionally a hint of temper. He started off by winning the New Stakes at Ascot and then a minor event at Stockbridge, but in the autumn he went under by a head to St Gris in the Imperial Produce Stakes at Kempton Park. Porter reckoned Flying Fox had been unlucky and would retrieve his reputation in the Middle Park Plate, but that race was run at a muddling pace in a howling gale and Flying Fox managed to get beaten by the American-bred Caiman ridden by Tod Sloan. Sloan's style of riding offered far less wind resistance than did that of Flying Fox's partner Mornington Cannon who sat upright in the traditional English manner that Sloan and other American jockeys were beginning to make look ridiculous. A fortnight after the Middle Park, Flying Fox won his final race of the season, the

Flying Fox, 1899, by Emil Adam. (The Jockey Club, Newmarket)

Criterion Stakes at Newmarket.

Flying Fox wintered well and was well tried before the Guineas which he won comfortably enough in the end, but not before he had shortened the life expectancy of some of his more confident supporters. This was before the starting-gate was in operation and time again, when the flag was up, Flying Fox bolted away into the open country on the left. It looked as if he would never get off but the starter showed patience almost beyond the call of duty and eventually got him under away. As Flying Fox passed the winning-post, the Duke, usually the most dignified and reserved of patricians, let loose an ear-splitting 'View Hulloa' which greatly shocked the stuffier members of the private stand. In fact there was more talk afterwards about the Duke's yell of triumph than about the manner of Flying Fox's victory.

Caiman, second in the Guineas, did not compete in the Derby which was reckoned to be virtually a match between Flying Fox, the 5–2 on favourite, and the French colt Holocauste, a 6–1 chance

ridden by Sloan. Approaching Tattenham Corner, Flying Fox moved up to join Holocauste, a big, powerful grey. With 2 furlongs to go Cannon was niggling at the favourite whereas Sloan had not moved on Holocauste. Suddenly there was a noise like a pistol-shot and the grey staggered and fell. He had broken a fetlock, and according to Sloan 'the stump was sticking into the ground'. He had to be destroyed on the course and Flying Fox won at his leisure. Sloan, of course, said he would have won, but in fact his opinion was backed by George Lambton and by Mr Arthur Coventry, the starter. It was the Duke's fourth Derby winner and the seventh for Porter who retired in 1905.

After the Derby, Flying Fox won the Princess of Wales's Stakes at Newmarket, the Eclipse Stakes and finally the St Leger in which he beat Caiman by three lengths. That was the last race of his career and he had won over £40000 in stakes. Porter had no desire to train him as a four-year-old in view of his temperament, and following the Duke's death he was sold to M. Edmond Blanc for 37500 gns, a

Diamond Jubilee, 1900, by Emil Adam. (The Jockey Club, Newmarket)

price at the time thought wildly excessive. In fact M. Blanc secured a bargain as Flying Fox did extremely well as a sire. M. Blanc exercised a 'closed shop' principle that did not greatly endear him to other breeders. Flying Fox's services were not available to French breeders at all, while there was a fee of 600 gns for foreign mares who had to leave France before they foaled. Teddy, by Flying Fox's son Ajax that won the Grand Prix de Paris for M. Blanc, founded influential sires lines in France, Italy and America; among his offspring were Sir Gallahad III, Asterus, Ortello, a great sire in Italy, and Bull Dog, sire of Bull Lea; to say nothing of the Oaks winner Rose of England, dam of the St Leger winner Chulmleigh. Sir Gallahad III was four times champion sire in America and eleven times leading sire of successful brood-mares. Bull Dog was Sir Gallahad III's full brother and his record as a sire in America was almost as good. Bull Lea was five times champion sire in America. Asterus was champion sire in France in 1934 and leading sire of brood-mares there 6 years in succession.

DIAMOND JUBILEE (1900)

The year 1900 was a marvellous one for the Prince of Wales (later King Edward VII). Not only did he win the Triple Crown with Diamond Jubilee, but he also won the Grand National with Ambush II.

There have been better Triple Crown winners than Diamond Jubilee: few, if any, more handsome; certainly none worse-tempered. In fact his savage temper at one point threatened to wreck his career and his achievements form a lasting tribute to the skill and patience of his trainer Richard Marsh; and to the pluck and perseverance of his hitherto almost unknown rider Herbert Jones.

Foaled in the 60th year of Queen Victoria's reign, Diamond Jubilee, a bright bay, was by St Simon out of Perdita II and was thus a brother of the 1896 Derby winner, Persimmon. Because of that relationship, and because he was exceptionally good-looking, he was the subject of too much fussing and petting in his early days. Partially at least on account of that, he became like a spoiled child, peevish and perverse when he did not get his own way. He possessed a streak of arrogance, too, and in Marsh's words: 'He would walk straight at you, and over you if you did not give way.' It was impossible not to admire him, though, and Marsh rated him the only perfectly formed thoroughbred, impossible to fault, he had ever seen. Lord Chaplin, who had owned the Derby winner Hermit and was a notable judge of a horse, endorsed that view.

Diamond Jubilee soon showed that he possessed high ability, and following a thoroughly satisfactory trial he was confidently expected to emulate Persimmon and win the Coventry Stakes at Royal Ascot. In the paddock at Ascot, Marsh was just telling Sir Dighton Probyn what a thoroughly nice colt Diamond Jubilee was when Diamond Jubilee lashed out and kicked an unfortunate bystander. Down at the start Diamond Jubilee was either walking about on his hind legs or doing his best to eat his jockey, Jack Watts. Watts was by nature placid and reserved, and when he subsequently told Marsh just what he thought of Diamond Jubilee, Marsh got quite a shock. The starter, Mr Arthur Coventry, said he had never seen a two-year-old behave quite so badly. Diamond Jubilee did eventually start but finished down the course.

On his return home Diamond Jubilee behaved with faultless decorum both in the stable and out on the Heath, and Marsh began to hope that the Ascot fiasco might be just an isolated incident. Diamond Jubilee walked quietly down to the July course for the July Stakes for which he was favourite. Unfortunately, the less agreeable side of his character then became evident. He unseated Watts and galloped off down the course. He was captured and remounted but declined to exert himself in the race and finished last.

Naturally there were plenty of people to advise the Prince of Wales, his racing manager Lord Marcus Beresford, and Marsh on the treatment Diamond Jubilee required. 'A damned good hiding' was the most frequent suggestion, but Marsh realised that though strong-arm methods might eventually subdue Diamond Jubilee, they would probably break his spirit completely as well and render him utterly useless. There is a story, though, that at one point in Diamond Jubilee's career his conduct was so objectionable that it was reluctantly decided to cut him. However, the vet who was to carry out the operation discovered Diamond Jubilee was a one-sided rig and so nothing was done.

It was clear that Diamond Jubilee hated Jack Watts, so in the Prince of Wales's Stakes at Goodwood he was partnered by Mornington Cannon. Diamond Jubilee behaved and ran much better than previously, finishing second to Epsom Lad, a gelding that won the Eclipse Stakes at four. In the autumn, again ridden by Cannon, Diamond Jubilee won the Boscowen Stakes at Newmarket, but the opposition was not of great account. In the Middle Park Plate Cannon was not available, but Diamond Jubilee went quite well for Watts and finished close up second to Democratic who eventually became Lord Kitchener's charger in India. On what he had accomplished at two, there were no grounds for forecasting resounding triumphs for Diamond Jubilee the following season.

During the winter Marsh kept Diamond Jubilee busy to stop him getting above himself, and in his work Diamond Jubilee was usually ridden by a lad named Herbert Jones, whose father Jack Jones had once trained jumpers for the Prince and Lord Marcus Beresford. Herbert Jones took immense trouble with Diamond Jubilee and got on with him better than anyone else.

In early April Mornington Cannon came down to Newmarket to ride Diamond Jubilee. When the work was over he dismounted and led Diamond Jubilee by the bridle. Quite suddenly Diamond Jubilee attacked him, rolled him over and would have killed him if help had not been at hand. Not surprisingly Cannon was badly shaken. Just before the Guineas Cannon again rode Diamond Jubilee. Marsh thought the horse had gone extremely well: Cannon on the other hand said Diamond Jubilee would not go for him and suggested another jockey be engaged. It is not hard to understand Cannon's point of view. It was not easy to find a suitable jockey at such short notice, and in the end it was decided to take a chance and put Jones up. The experiment was a success and starting at 11–4, Diamond Jubilee won the Two Thousand Guineas by four lengths. He followed that up by winning the Newmarket Stakes, though only by a head from Chevening.

In the interval between the Guineas and the Derby Diamond Jubilee's conduct at home was unpredictable. Some mornings he spent dancing around on his hind legs; on others he stood stock-still and refused to budge. Luckily, on Derby Day he was on his best behaviour. Favourite at 6–4 and ridden with flawless judgement by Jones, he ran on with admirable resolution to beat Simon Dale by a length and a half. The Prince was given a tremendous reception, but it perhaps lacked the wholly spontaneous warmth of the reception he received after the victory of Persimmon.

At Newmarket in July Diamond Jubilee was fairly and squarely beaten by a smart filly called Merry Gal to whom he was endeavouring to concede 19 lb in the Princess of Wales's Stakes. However, he won the Eclipse Stakes, then a far more valuable race than the Derby, giving 10 lb to

Chevening who had run him so close in the Newmarket Stakes.

Before the St Leger Diamond Jubilee was in a truly devilish mood. It took Marsh 20 minutes to get a saddle on his back, and at the end of that period it was hard to say which of the two was sweating the more profusely. Diamond Jubilee's advance towards the starting-gate was conducted on his hind legs, but he was well enough away and won comfortably from Elopement. His price was the unrewarding one of 7–2 on. He was never as good again after the St Leger and seemed to have burnt himself out. He failed in the Jockey Club Stakes that autumn and he did not win the following season. He was retired to the Sandringham Stud at a fee of 300 gns, having won over £29 000 in stakes, largely due to the skill of Marsh and the courage of Jones. Towards the end of 1900 Jones had been utterly exhausted, both physically and mentally, and Marsh sent him off to Brighton to recuperate.

At Sandringham Diamond Jubilee was a demon to start with but eventually settled down. In 1906 he was sold for £31 500 to a South American breeder. He proved a great success in Argentina where he died at the ripe age of 26.

SPEARMINT (1906)

The best of the American jockeys riding here between 1900 and the outbreak of the First World War was Danny Maher, a man of notable charm and intelligence. He always reckoned that with the possible exception of Bayardo, Spearmint was the best horse he ever rode in this country. Spearmint was the last English-trained colt to bring off the Derby–Grand Prix double. In recent years the Grand Prix has declined sharply in value and prestige. It is now thought that a midsummer race over a distance just short of 2 miles, often run in very hot weather, imposes too great a strain on a three-year-old and the Grand Prix is now rated far less important than the Prix du Jockey Club. In Spearmint's day, though, it was unquestionably the race of the year in France.

Spearmint was bred by Sir Tatton Sykes at Sledmere and was a bay colt by Carbine out of Maid of the Mint, by the Grand Prix winner Minting. Carbine, bred in New Zealand, was just about the most famous horse ever to race in Australia, his outstanding performance being to win the Melbourne Cup from 38 opponents carrying 10 st 5 and conceding 53 lb to the runner-up. In New Zealand poker-players are still apt to call a hand containing a pair of tens and a pair of fives a 'Carbine' in memory of the weight carried on that celebrated occasion.

In 1895 the Duke of Portland, wanting an outcross for his St Simon and Donovan mares, bought Carbine for 13 000 gns. In England Carbine sired plenty of smart handicappers, but Spearmint was his only top-class winner. The 1928 Derby winner Felstead had three lines of Carbine blood in his pedigree: his dam had been bought in foal to Spearmint's son Spion Kop by the Lambourn trainer Captain O M D Bell, who was by birth an Australian.

Shortly before the 1904 Doncaster yearling sales Major Eustace Loder, who had served for 15 years in the 12th Lancers and who owned that magnificent mare Pretty Polly, visited the Sledmere Stud accompanied by his stud manager Mr Noble Johnson, renowned as an exceptional judge of a horse. At all events they both took a great liking to Spearmint, despite the fact that he was light of bone and his forelegs were certainly open to criticism, and they were determined to buy him. They were able to obtain him for 300 gns partly because a good many people doubted if he would stand training; partly because there was no great demand for Carbine's stock. Soon after reaching Peter Gilpin's stable at Newmarket, Spearmint developed a fever that he could not throw off for 5 months. Speaking of this illness after Spearmint had won the Derby, Gilpin observed: 'The miracle is not that he should be worth thousands, but so much as half a sovereign.'

At two Spearmint's record was no more than ordinary. He won the Great Foal Plate at Lingfield by a head from mediocre opposition. He was third to the brilliant but quite unpredictable Black Arrow at Derby, and fourth with top weight in the Richmond Nursery at Newmarket. He was rated considerably inferior to a couple of two-year-old stable-companions, Major Loder's Admirable Crichton, a half-brother to Pretty Polly, and Sir Daniel Cooper's filly Flair, by St Frusquin. The following season Admirable Crichton failed to train on, but Flair won the One Thousand Guineas with such impressive ease that it was decided that she alone would represent Gilpin's stable in the Derby, Spearmint being reserved for the Grand Prix. This plan, however, was knocked on the head when Flair broke down badly soon after her Newmarket triumph. It was then decreed that Spearmint would take his chance in the Derby. There were no fears of his ability to stay as Carbine was a stayer while Maid of the Mint, who never ran herself, was a half-sister to the Cesarewitch winner Wargrave. In the meantime Spearmint worked so well with Pretty Polly and the Cesarewitch winner Hammerkop (subsequently the dam of Spion Kop who won the 1920 Derby for Major (later Lieutenant Colonel) Giles Loder) that his price contracted from 20–1 to 6–1.

Spearmint, 1906, by Emil Adam. (The Jockey Club, Newmarket)

Favourite for the Derby was Lally owned by Captain W B Purefoy, generally rated the shrewdest member of the famous Druids Lodge 'confederacy'. Lally, though, was by no means sure to stay the distance. Spearmint was second favourite at 6–1. Also in the field were Troutbeck, who was to win the St Leger and whose only defeat at three was in the Derby; and those fine stayers The White Knight and Radium, the former the future winner of the Coronation Cup and the Gold Cup twice, the latter of the Goodwood Cup and the Doncaster Cup.

Lally was ridden by the erratic Bernard Dillon who, 8 years later, became the third husband of that star of the Music Halls, Marie Lloyd. Lally was very badly away and Dillon made up the lost ground with such impetuosity that Lally was a spent force by half-way. At Tattenham Corner Troutbeck and Picton disputed the lead, Picton being ridden by the accomplished amateur Mr George Thursby. Spearmint was hard on their heels, though, and with 2 furlongs to go the three were in line. Just inside the distance Picton got his head in front, and for a few strides it really looked as if an amateur was going to

win the Derby, but then Maher showed Spearmint the whip and Spearmint lengthened his stride to win by a length and a half from Picton with Troutbeck third. The time of 2 min 36⅘ s beat the record established by Cicero.

Only 11 days later Spearmint lined up for the Grand Prix. Cheered on by a strong force of English supporters, he beat Brisecoeur by a neck. The English fairly let themselves go in Paris that night, and one of Major Loder's nephews danced a cancan in the Jardin de Paris with a senior member of the chorus who was estimated to be over 50 years of age and to tip the scales at 18 st.

After those two triumphs Spearmint developed leg trouble and never raced again. He was retired to his owner's stud in County Kildare at a fee of 250 gns. He did not prove an outstanding success, his best winners being Spion Kop (Derby), Royal Lancer (St Leger) and Zionist (Irish Derby). He also sired that famous mare Plucky Liège, dam of Bois Roussel (Derby), Admiral Drake (Grand Prix) and Sir Gallahad III, a top-class racehorse and an extremely successful sire.

ORBY (1907)

Derby winners trained in Ireland are common enough nowadays. There was not one, though, in the last century and the very first was Orby in 1907. Orby was bred and owned by a Mr Richard Croker. Some singularly unattractive individuals have owned Derby winners—few more so than Croker. Irish by birth, he had emigrated to America as a child. Thick-set, uncouth of features and of speech, self-opinionated and ruthless, he was a corrupt New York politician, the Boss of Tammany Hall. When at long last matters became rather too warm for him in New York, he transferred himself and his extremely large fortune to England. He bought himself a place in Berkshire and decided to take up racing. His operations on the Turf cost him a lot of money to start with as he held firmly to the view that American horses were vastly superior to English ones. Eventually though, he saw the light and established the Glencairn Stud in Ireland where Orby, foaled in England, was reared.

Orby was by Orme, sire of the Triple Crown winner Flying Fox, out of Rhoda B, by Hanover. Rhoda B was imported from America as a yearling in 1896, and she would have been ineligible for inclusion in the General Stud Book prior to a GSB ruling of 1901. She also bred Rhodora who won the One Thousand Guineas. Rhodora was incestuously mated with her half-brother Orby with disastrous result.

In England Croker's horses had been trained at Wantage by Charles Morton. In Ireland Croker appointed Colonel Frederick McCabe as his trainer and general racing manager. McCabe was an able and extremely versatile man with highly original

Orby, 1907. (*The British Racehorse*)

views on most subjects including the training of racehorses. He was a qualified doctor and in his youth had achieved some distinction as a cross-country runner and cyclist. He gave up a flourishing Dublin practice to serve in the South African War as medical officer to the South Irish Horse. In later years he had a variety of commercial interests and in addition owned and edited a number of publications. He died in 1954, aged 86.

At two Orby ran twice in Ireland, starting favourite and finishing third on each occasion. The following season he had two races before the Derby, the Earl of Sefton Plate at Liverpool and the Baldoyle Plate at Baldoyle, winning them both with ease. These victories, coupled with persistent reports of his progress, resulted in him being soundly backed for the Derby at 100–9. Few, though, seriously believed him capable of beating Captain Henry Greer's Slieve Gallion who had been a top-class two-year-old and who had won the Two Thousand Guineas impressively. At Epsom Slieve Gallion, ridden by W. Higgs, started at 13–8 on.

Slieve Gallion was in front at Tattenham Corner, but he did not stay the distance and 2 furlongs out he lost his action and began to veer sharply towards the stands. Orby, ridden by the American jockey Johnny Reiff, then took the lead, but he was not a true stayer either and he began to change his legs and hang to the right. In the meantime Wool Winder, who for some reason had dropped back to last coming down the hill, was making ground up fast. Orby, though, had too long a lead and held on to win by two lengths with Slieve Gallion third. There were some disobliging rumours afterwards concerning Otto Madden and his riding of Wool Winder who subsequently won the St Leger. Wool Winder belonged to Brigadier E W Baird who had won the 1886 Grand National with his half-bred hunter Playfair and who was a member of the Jockey Club for 64 years.

There were hectic scenes of jubilation among the Irish present when Orby won, but Reiff put a damper on the rejoicings by saying that it was a poor Derby field and there were several better three-year-olds than Orby in France. Reiff had come to this country at the turn of the century as a dear little innocent boy in a knickerbocker suit and an Eton collar—the look of innocence, though, was deceptive.

Orby won the Irish Derby in a canter but was last of four in a race at Liverpool. He was examined by a vet who prescribed rest. Nevertheless, he was trained for the St Leger, broke down before that race and never ran again. The best winners he sired were the 1919 Derby victor Grand Parade and that very fast and extremely courageous filly Diadem

who won the One Thousand Guineas. The Orby male-line survived, however, not through Grand Parade but through The Boss who won six races worth £1584. The Boss sired Sir Cosmo who in turn sired the sprinter and successful sire Panorama, while another son of The Boss, Golden Boss, sired the brilliant sprinter and successful sire Gold Bridge. Golden Boss was sold as a remount sire to America before Gold Bridge's merits had become known.

Stories about Colonel McCabe form part of the lore and legend of Irish racing. Apparently the Colonel maintained his connection with the South Irish Horse after the war was over. The regiment was in camp at the time of Orby's triumph and the Commanding Officer received a telegram stating: 'Medical Officer authorises the issue of champagne to all ranks.' The celebrations that night are said to have been of a memorable nature.

SUNSTAR (1911)

There were few owners more consistently successful between the turn of the century and the early 1920s than Mr Jack Barnato Joel, a shrewd man of humble origin who had made a vast fortune in South Africa. He won eleven Classic races, and these successes included two winners of the Derby.

There was drama over both these Derby wins. Sunstar had broken down just before the race and literally won on three legs and a 'swinger'. Humorist, a horse of remarkable courage, was suffering from a tubercular lung condition when he won at Epsom, and he suffered a fatal haemorrhage a fortnight later.

On the face of it Sunstar, bred by his owner, hardly seemed to possess a Derby pedigree. His sire Sundridge, by Amphion, was touched in his wind but rose from competing in selling races to being a high-class sprinter. He won the six furlongs July Cup three years running, each time with 10 st 2. His original stud fee was 9 gns but he rose to be champion sire. Doris, Sunstar's dam, was by Loved One. She was only a little pony and never rose above selling plates. She had formerly belonged to Mr 'Solly' Joel who held a low opinion of her and let his brother have her for nothing. She also bred Princess Dorrie, winner of the One Thousand Guineas and the Oaks.

Mr Joel's trainer was the very experienced Charles Morton who had learnt the business from that remarkable character Tom Parr. Before he entered the racing world, Parr had been a travelling tea-pedlar operating between Weymouth and Plymouth. Parr found difficulty in establishing himself as a trainer and often had to hide in the hayloft while his head-lad kept creditors at bay. In due course, though, his stable won many races and Morton retained a high opinion of his professional ability.

As a two-year-old Sunstar gave Morton few grounds for thinking he would ever attain Classic standard. However, to offset a number of reverses he did win the International Plate at Kempton Park and the Exeter Stakes at Newmarket, while he dead-heated with the speedy Borrow in the Hopeful Stakes at Newmarket. During the winter he thrived and Morton soon realised he had made quite exceptional improvement. On Good Friday morning, in the presence of his owner, he did a remarkably good gallop against thoroughly reliable trial-horses and from that moment it was clear that he was going to take a lot of beating in the Classics.

Ridden by the French jockey George Stern, who never set eyes on Sunstar before seeing him in the paddock at Newmarket, Sunstar won the Two Thousand Guineas easily from Lord Derby's Stedfast and his own stable-companion Lycaon. A fortnight later he won the mile and a quarter Newmarket Stakes. The critics were not much impressed by that victory, but Stern told Morton that Sunstar had run idly and had won with a lot in hand.

It was a dry spring and the gallops at Wantage became extremely hard. This was worrying for Morton as Sunstar was a hot favourite for the Derby and Mr Joel and his friends stood to win a fortune in bets. Eight days before the Epsom meeting began, the blow fell. After a mile and a quarter gallop Sunstar pulled up dead lame, having severely strained a suspensory ligament. Morton kept cool at this moment of crisis. The other horses were some distance away so he got hold of Sunstar's lad and promised him a nice present if he kept his

Sunstar, 1911. (*The British Racehorse*)

mouth shut: nothing, or worse than nothing, if he talked. He then rang up Mr Joel and told him that Sunstar was so fit that he might be able to run if the actual lameness could be dispersed: but that if Sunstar did run, he would certainly never race again.

What Morton did not know about horses' legs was hardly worth the bother of finding out. He had no need to spend money on vets whenever any little thing went wrong as he was quite capable of coping with the situation himself. For a week, he hardly left Sunstar's side and eventually the lameness was got rid of. Inevitably news of Sunstar's trouble leaked out. The bookmakers started to lay him freely: Mr Joel retaliated by backing him. All sorts of rumours were in circulation and it was said that the bookmakers had 'got at' Sunstar because they could not afford to let him win. There was a story, too, of a plot to put Stern over the rails during the descent to Tattenham Corner. This caused even the sorely troubled Morton to smile as of all the jockeys of that era Stern was just about the toughest, well capable not only of self-preservation but of carrying out highly effective reprisals.

Despite everything, Sunstar was favourite at 13–8. It was a close, sultry afternoon and tempers were liable to be short. On his way to the course, Morton tripped up, injured his shoulder and in consequence could not saddle Sunstar. A large and somewhat unruly crowd collected down by the start and Stedfast became upset. When the gate went up he whipped round and lost 100 yd. In the race Sunstar was always well placed and seemed to be going smoothly. There was a very nasty moment in the straight when he suddenly faltered, but Stern got him balanced again and Sunstar recovered to win decisively by two lengths from Stedfast who had made up an immense amount of ground in the straight.

Morton had been quite right. Sunstar was so lame when he pulled up that he could hardly walk back to the unsaddling enclosure. He never ran again. His victory owed much to his own pluck and to Morton's professional expertise. As a sire he did well, his stock winning 440 races worth £229 000. His record would have been even better but for the war. Among his winners were Sunny Jane (Oaks), Buchan (second in the Derby, twice winner of the

Sansovino, 1924, by Cecil Wilson. (The Jockey Club, Newmarket)

Eclipse Stakes, champion sire), Craig an Eran (Two Thousand Guineas, second in the Derby, sire of the Derby winner April the Fifth and the Grand Prix de Paris winner Admiral Drake) and Galloper Light (Grand Prix de Paris). Sunstar was twice leading sire of brood-mares. At one point in his stud career there was a rumpus because breeders complained he was being allowed to cover too many mares. In fact he was an exceptionally virile horse and his exertions did him no harm. When he died aged 18 he was reputed to have left more foals than any other sire this century.

SANSOVINO (1924)

In 1787 the 12th Earl of Derby won the Derby with Sir Peter Teazle named in compliment to his second wife, Elizabeth Farren. Despite liberal patronage of the Turf, the Stanley family was not able to repeat that success for 137 years. The winner on this second occasion was Sansovino, bred and owned by the 17th Earl, a man whose long life was devoted to the service of his country. As regards racing, he was an owner–breeder of the type that once formed the backbone of the sport in this country but since the Second World War has almost ceased to exist. Immensely successful, he won 20 Classic races including the Derby with Sansovino, Hyperion and Watling Street, and for many years there were few important races without a representative carrying the famous and popular 'black jacket, white cap'. It is probably true to say that his influence on bloodstock-breeding throughout the world has never been equalled.

Sansovino was a big, powerful bay by his owner's St Leger winner Swynford, who was fortunately saved for the stud after smashing a fetlock joint as a four-year-old while doing a half-speed gallop. Dam of Sansovino was Gondolette, one of the most famous mares in the General Stud Book. By Loved One out of Dongola, by Doncaster, she was sold as a yearling for 75 gns to Mr George Edwardes of Gaiety Theatre fame for whom she was a very modest winner. He resold her at three for 360 gns to Colonel W. Hall-Walker (later Lord Wavertree) for whom she bred Great Sport and Let Fly, both placed in the Derby, and Dolabella, dam of the brilliant Myrobella who bred the Two Thousand Guineas winner Big Game and whose descendants include the St Leger winner Chamossaire and the Derby winner Snow Knight.

Lord Derby bought Gondolette as a ten-year-old for 1550 gns, the main reason for the purchase being that Loved One was by See Saw out of Pilgrimage, and Lord Derby wished to mate Gondolette with either Chaucer or Swynford, both grandsons of

Pilgrimage. Gondolette bred six winners for Lord Derby, the most notable besides Sansovino being Ferry, who won the One Thousand Guineas, and Serenissima. A daughter of Minoru, Serenissima bred eight winners of 40 races, among them Selene who won over £14 000 herself and became the dam of Hyperion.

Trained by George Lambton at Newmarket, Sansovino ran twice at two and proved that he had plenty of speed by winning the Richmond Stakes at Goodwood and the Gimcrack Stakes at York. In neither case, however, was the opposition particularly strong. It is interesting to note that by those two victories Sansovino earned £2828: the combined value of the two races in 1978 was over £42 000.

Perhaps because it had been reckoned that staying would be Sansovino's game, he was never entered for the Two Thousand Guineas. His first race at three was the Rugeley Stakes at Birmingham in April. Starting at 5–1 on, he scraped home by inches from the four-year-old Rugeley, and the critics were singularly unimpressed. However, he was very backward at the time and the form looked distinctly better when Rugeley won the Chester Cup the following month.

Sansovino's next race, his final one before the Derby, was the mile and a quarter Newmarket Stakes. This race was run at a muddling pace and Sansovino finished third, a neck and a head behind Hurstwood and Salmon Trout, with Bright Knight, a stable-companion of Hurstwood at Manton, a head away fourth. Bright Knight had been beaten a short head by Diophon in the Two Thousand Guineas and almost everyone at Newmarket bar the judge was convinced he had won. Lambton was satisfied with Sansovino's running. The poor pace had not helped such a genuine stayer, and in addition Sansovino had been badly hampered at one stage.

It was clear to Lambton that Sansovino was making rapid and striking improvement and as Derby Day approached his confidence increased. In his final gallop Sansovino was opposed by two high-class four-year-olds: Tranquil, winner of the One Thousand Guineas and the St Leger; and Pharos, who had been close up second in the Derby. Receiving only 3 lb, Sansovino slammed them by half a dozen lengths. On that form he really did look something to bet on. In fact, one jockey who had ridden in the gallop hurried off home, and after collecting and pawning his wife's jewellery, he put every penny he had been able to raise on Sansovino. Naturally, news of this splendid gallop soon became public: money poured on to Sansovino and in the end he started favourite at 9–2.

On the Saturday and Sunday before the Derby it

rained continuously, and in some parts of the country 4 in fell within 36 hours. The Epsom course became desperately heavy, but this did not worry Lambton who was certain that Sansovino had the strength and the stamina to cope with the most testing conditions. On Derby Day it started raining at midday and continued raining throughout the night. The course simply could not absorb this fresh downpour and by the time the big race was run the track was in a fearful condition. On the Downs there was a scene of desolation: buses and cars sank up to their axles in the mud and many, unable to move, remained there till dragged out the following morning. On the Thursday a part of the straight course near Tattenham Corner where traffic passed over was a quagmire, and two 5-furlong races had to be abandoned. The Epsom executive was subjected to searing criticism for lack of energy and initiative in coping with the situation, and the Jockey Club was moved to appoint a Committee of Inquiry.

The miserable conditions were no inconvenience to Sansovino. Tommy Weston took him to the front coming down the hill to Tattenham Corner, and from then on the issue was never in doubt. Sansovino never looked like stopping and he passed the post six lengths in front of St Germans with Hurstwood third. St Germans belonged to Lord Astor and was his fifth Derby runner-up in 7 years.

Sansovino's victory was extremely popular and Lord Derby, beaming with happiness and in total disregard of the pelting rain, was given a tremendous reception as he led his colt in. An hour after the race the 21-year-old Weston was sharing a wooden horse with his wife on a merry-go-round on the Downs.

None the worse for his Epsom exertions, Sansovino ran twice at Royal Ascot, winning the Prince of Wales's Stakes and finishing unplaced behind Chosroes in the Hardwicke Stakes. He was coughing not long before Doncaster, and Lambton did not wish to run him in the St Leger, but Lord Derby insisted on giving ante-post backers a run for their money. Sansovino was unplaced behind Salmon Trout. At four Sansovino had leg trouble and never found his best form. He did, however, beat the Two Thousand Guineas winner Diophon over a mile at Lingfield. Among the races he failed to win was the City and Suburban: no Derby winner has run in that popular Epsom handicap since.

As a stallion Sansovino was hardly the success anticipated. The best horse he sired was Sandwich who won the 1931 St Leger for Lord Rosebery and was probably a very unlucky loser of the Derby. Among Sansovino's daughters was Sansonnet, dam of the brilliant Tudor Minstrel. Two of Sansovino's sons, St Magnus and Portofino, did well as sires in Australia.

HYPERION (1933)

Few great racehorses capture the affection of the public to the extent that Hyperion did. There were two reasons for this. Firstly, he was only a little fellow and seemed to be battling against physical odds; secondly, he was so obviously a character with an individuality of his own.

Bred by his owner, the 17th Earl of Derby, Hyperion stood well under 15 hands when he joined George Lambton's stable. When he won the Derby he stood 15 hands $1\frac{1}{2}$ in and was the smallest winner of the race since Little Wonder, who was strongly suspected of being a four-year-old, 93 years previously. A chestnut with four white socks and a head clearly denoting intelligence and courage, Hyperion was in fact beautifully made. His lack of inches were deceptive as his length and depth were those of a considerably taller horse: it was the shortness of his cannon-bones that brought him so near to the ground. He was by Gainsborough, winner of a wartime Triple Crown, out of Selene, by Chaucer out of Serenissima. Selene was small but she was tough and game and a high-class race-mare winning 15 races, dead-heating in another and earning over £14 000 in stakes. Chaucer, described by George Lambton as 'a little pony' inherited his lack of inches from his dam Canterbury Pilgrim who won the Oaks. However, if some of Hyperion's ancestors were on the small side, there was no shortage of racing ability.

As a foal Hyperion was not only small but weakly and at one point there was even talk about putting him down. His physique gradually improved, but on account of his size he was not sent into training with Lord Derby's other yearlings; and he would probably have been sold if George Lambton, a wonderful judge with a deep understanding of horses, had not taken a liking to him. For a considerable time it looked as if Lambton had picked a loser as Hyperion's work at home was singularly unimpressive. In his first race, the £162 Zetland Maiden Plate at Doncaster, he started at 25–1 and Lambton did not even go and see him run. On the racecourse, Hyperion was fortunately a far livelier performer than he was on the home gallops, and he finished a creditable fourth in a big field. Lambton was not yet convinced of Hyperion's merit but lingering doubts were swept away when the little chestnut won the New Stakes at Ascot by three lengths from Nun's Veil who was destined to be the fourth dam of the 1964 Derby winner Santa Claus. It was a mating between Hyperion and Nun's Veil's daughter Clarence that produced the triple Classic winner Sun Chariot.

In his next two races Hyperion failed to reproduce the speed and dash he had shown at Ascot

Hyperion, 1933. (*The British Racehorse*)

where he had covered the stiff 5 furlongs in 61 s, a slightly faster time than that taken by the three-year-old sprinter Gold Bridge the same afternoon. At Goodwood he was only able to dead-heat in the Prince of Wales's Stakes with the Nancy Stair filly, while in the Boscawen Stakes at Newmarket in September he was a poor third of four behind Manitoba. His last race that season was the seven furlongs Dewhurst Stakes at Newmarket. He had been working sluggishly at home and was displaying little enthusiasm in the race when Tommy Weston gave him a sharp reminder with the whip approaching the Bushes. This produced the desired result as Hyperion immediately accelerated and ran on strongly up the hill to win by two lengths with the odds-on favourite Felicitation fourth. This performance justified the hope that Hyperion might prove a Derby horse in 1933.

Hyperion had not been entered for the Guineas. His first race was the mile and a half Chester Vase,

and in winning by two lengths on heavy ground Hyperion resolved any doubts that might have existed about his stamina. Meanwhile, his work at home was so unimpressive that his Derby price drifted to 10–1, though in fact he eventually started favourite at 6–1. He was accompanied to the post at Epsom by Lord Derby's Thrapston, Donoghue up, to act as pacemaker. Donoghue, a truly great Epsom rider, did his job to perfection, setting a fast pace but not an absurd one. Furthermore he left room for Hyperion and Weston to come up on the inside approaching Tattenham Corner. The stable-companions rounded the bend together. Soon afterwards Weston gave Hyperion one tap with the whip, and Hyperion strode away in magnificent style to win by four lengths from King Salmon. The time of 2 min 34 s established a new record.

At Ascot Hyperion won the Prince of Wales's Stakes, then run over 1 mile and 5 furlongs. In July he suffered a slight dislocation of the stifle-joint and had to miss the race named after him at Hurst Park. At one point his St Leger price went out to 20–1 but the injury soon mended and he won the St Leger without ever being extended by three lengths from Felicitation. The French Derby winner Thor II finished 13th.

A season of triumph ended on a sad note. Possibly the trouble began when Lambton had a nasty fall at home in May and in consequence was unable to travel to Epsom to saddle Hyperion for the Derby. Lord Derby apparently took the view that it was time for Lambton, then aged 73, to retire and terminated his contract as private trainer from the end of the season, appointing Colledge Leader as his successor.

It is fair to say that the able and conscientious Leader never really understood Hyperion as Lambton did and at times was rather too tender with him. Certainly, Hyperion was not an easy horse to deal with. Apart from his habitual indolence, he had one or two eccentricities like deciding to stand still for half an hour or more on the Heath and resolutely declining to move. He clearly enjoyed attracting attention, and in several harmless little ways he was accustomed to play to the gallery. Leader certainly seemed to under-estimate the amount of work Hyperion would need to get him fit for the Gold Cup, his main objective. Hyperion won the ten furlongs March Stakes at Newmarket rather unimpressively and then the mile and a half Burwell Stakes, also at Newmarket. It was not long before the Gold Cup that he did his first 2-mile gallop and in this he became so distressed that Weston pulled him up.

News of this fiasco soon spread round Newmarket, and particular note of it was taken by Frank Butters whose Gold Cup candidate was the Aga Khan's Felicitation. Butters believed in putting his stayers through the mill and if they could stand up to this treatment they lacked nothing on the score of fitness. The day before the Cup Felicitation ran in the two miles Churchill Stakes and won by ten lengths. In the Cup he was partnered by Gordon Richards who was ordered to set off in front and test Hyperion's stamina to the utmost. Felicitation almost galloped poor little Hyperion to a standstill and won by eight lengths from Thor II with Hyperion a very weary third. It was a terrible disappointment to Lord Derby and to all Hyperion's admirers. Nor did Hyperion's next race, which proved to be his final one, bring consolation. In the mile and a half Dullingham Stakes at Newmarket he was beaten a short head by his solitary opponent, Lord Rosebery's Caithness, to whom he was conceding 29 lb. Thus Hyperion's career ended in anticlimax. He was retired to the stud having earned £29 509 in prize-money, less

than the runner-up in the Derby receives today.

It would take too long to recapitulate in full all Hyperion's triumph as a sire. He was champion six times, a record surpassed only by St Simon, Stockwell and Hermit, second four times and once third. He was twice leading sire of brood-mares and five times second. His Classic winners were Godiva (One Thousand Guineas, Oaks), Owen Tudor (Derby), Sun Chariot (One Thousand Guineas, Oaks, St Leger), Sun Castle (St Leger), Hycilla (Oaks), Sun Stream (One Thousand Guineas, Oaks) and Hypericum (One Thousand Guineas). Good winners out of Hyperion mares included Parthia (Derby), Carrozza (Oaks), Alycidon (Gold Cup), Supertello (Gold Cup) and Fair Edith (Prix Vermeille, King George VI and Queen Elizabeth Stakes). His son Aureole, winner of the Coronation Cup and the King George VI and Queen Elizabeth Stakes, was twice champion sire here. Sons of Hyperion were champion in the United States, Australia, New Zealand, South Africa, Argentina, Belgium and Sweden.

In general Hyperion's daughters tended to be better than his sons. His offspring were often highly-strung and difficult—Sun Chariot and Aureole were typical examples—and required patience and careful handling. He himself continued to serve mares till he was 29 and died in 1960. Of all little horses he was probably the greatest.

BAHRAM (1935)

It has been said, no doubt with a great deal of truth, that the main interest in racing and breeding of the late Aga Khan was that of a dealer. His colours were carried by five winners of the Derby and sooner or later he sold them all. The best of the five was the Triple Crown winner Bahram. Often the Aga Khan expressed affection and admiration for Bahram, declaring that he would never sell him: but in due course he did, and for what now seems the absurdly low price of £40 000. Breeders in England and Ireland found it hard to forgive the Aga Khan for the export of Blenheim, Bahram and Mahmoud. The sales of My Love and Tulyar mattered a great deal less.

Bred at his owner's stud in County Kildare, Bahram was originally named Bahman, but Messrs Weatherby decreed he must be renamed to avoid the possibility of confusion with a horse called Barman. Bay in colour, he was by Blandford out of Friar's Daughter, by King George V's favourite horse, the sprinter Friar Marcus. Blandford was heavy topped and did not possess the best of joints. In consequence he was far from easy to train. He proved, though, an outstandingly successful sire

Bahram, 1935, by AG Haigh. (The Jockey Club, Newmarket)

and four of his sons—Trigo, Blenheim, Windsor Lad and Bahram—won the Derby. In addition he sired Brantôme, one of the best horses to race in France between the First and Second World Wars. In 1935, the year he died, Blandford was leading sire in both England and France.

Friar's Daughter had changed hands for 140 gns as a foal, and as a yearling Dick Dawson bought her on the Aga Khan's behalf for 250 gns, no doubt attracted by her being in-bred to St Simon. She was very small and only won a single race worth £168; but she bred seven winners in addition to Bahram, one of them being Dastur who won the Irish Derby and the Coronation Cup and was second in the Two Thousand Guineas, the Derby and the St Leger. Grandam of Friar's Daughter was the St Simon mare Concertina who bred the famous Plucky Liège, dam of the 1938 Derby winner Bois Roussel, Sir Gallahad III and Admiral Drake. Sir Gallahad III was four times champion sire in America, while Admiral Drake won the Grand Prix de Paris and

sired Phil Drake who, in 1955, brought off the Derby–Grand Prix double.

As a foal Bahram was somewhat delicate and for a time his lungs were affected following an attack of pneumonia. However, he recovered well and as a yearling looked full of promise. When fully grown he stood 16 hands 2 in and except for a rather skimpy tail was difficult to fault. Frank Butters, who in 1931 had succeeded Dawson as the Aga Khan's trainer, soon recognised his potential and was determined not to hurry him. In fact Bahram did not see a racecourse till July when he lined up for the five furlongs National Breeders Produce Stakes at Sandown, at that time the most valuable two-year-old prize of the season.

Bahram, Dick Perryman up, carried his owner's second colours, first colours being on Gordon Richards who rode Theft, winner of the Windsor Castle Stakes at Ascot and conceding Bahram 9 lb. From half-way the issue was between these two. Bahram, almost friendless in the market at 20–1, stuck to his task well and found a little bit extra close home to win by a neck. He had four more races that season—the Rous Memorial Stakes at Goodwood, the Gimcrack Stakes, the Boscawen (Post) Stakes at Newmarket and the Middle Park Stakes—and won them all. In these victories Bahram certainly did not dazzle those who saw him by his brilliance. Indolent by nature, he was averse to doing more than was absolutely necessary. He was placed top of the handicap Free Handicap with 9 st 7.

He thrived during the winter and his easy-going disposition made him an easy horse to handle. He was by no means reluctant to be the recipient of public admiration, and he was apt to receive visitors leaning against a wall in a self-satisfied manner with his front legs crossed. The Two Thousand Guineas was his first objective and it was planned to give him a preliminary outing in the Craven Stakes. Four days before that event, however, he ran a temperature, and though he recovered quickly it was thought prudent to give the race a miss. Despite his unbeaten record he had failed to impress a good many punters, and in the Guineas he started at 7–2, Bobsleigh being favourite at 7–4. Bobsleigh gave no trouble to Bahram who ran on stoutly up the hill to win by a length and a half from Theft.

Ridden again by Fred Fox, Bahram was a hot favourite for the Derby at 5–4. The one controversial feature of the race occurred a mile from home. Fox and Bahram were not at all well placed and Fox's attempts to make progress on the inside were proving fruitless. On the other hand Wragg on Theft was in an ideal position. Hearing a shout behind him, Wragg looked over his shoulder and saw Fox's plight. He at once pulled Theft out and Bahram slipped through to take Theft's place. This manœuvre was easily observable from the stands, and subsequently the stewards cautioned Wragg for a breach of Rule 139 which stated: *'Every horse which runs in a race shall run on his merits, whether his owner runs another horse in the race or not.'*

Bahram never looked like being beaten in the straight and won comfortably from Robin Goodfellow, later a successful sire in New Zealand, and Field Trial. By no stretch of the imagination could Bahram be said to have had a gruelling race, and it was decided to run him in the one mile St James's Palace Stakes at Ascot. He gave one of his most indolent performances and had to be pushed out to beat the moderate Portfolio by a length.

There was a long spell of dry weather that summer and with it came an epidemic of coughing. Bahram was coughing in August and had to miss the Hurst Park race planned for him. He was fit, though, in time for the St Leger in which he had only seven opponents. Ridden by Smirke, as Fox had

had a bad fall earlier at the meeting, and starting at 11–4 on, he won as he pleased from Solar Ray and Buckleigh.

He never ran again. Though he was perfectly sound and had had only nine races in two seasons, he was bustled away to the stud with a haste that verged on the indecent. The Aga Khan never subscribed to the view that the main function of a racehorse is to race. This premature retirement, coupled with his lack of panache in his manner of racing, did nothing to help Bahram's reputation. It was commonly stated that he had never beaten a good horse and was inferior to most other Triple Crown winners. He had, however, won from 5 furlongs to $1\frac{3}{4}$ miles, and as he had never been really extended it was hard to judge just how good he was. Frank Butters rated him the best horse he ever trained.

Bahram began his stud career in England at a fee of 500 gns. In this country he got the Two Thousand Guineas and Champion Stakes winner Big Game; Persian Gulf, who won the Coronation Cup and sired the 1959 Derby winner Parthia; and the St Leger winner Turkhan. He also sired the dams of Migoli (Eclipse Stakes and Prix de l'Arc de Triomphe), Elpenor (Gold Cup and Prix du Cadran) and Noor, a good winner both here and in America. In addition Mah Iran, dam of Migoli, was grandam of the brilliant Petite Étoile.

In 1940 the Aga Khan was said to be taking a disenchanted view on the outcome of the war, and he sold Bahram to an American syndicate for £40 000. Bahram was not in good health on arrival in the United States, and American breeders never really took to him. Five years later he was exported for $130 000 to Argentina where he was not a success. He died in 1956. His stud record would doubtless have been better had he stayed in England and not been subjected to changes of environment.

PINZA (1953)

In the 1953 Derby, sympathies were very much divided. The race was run on the Saturday of the week in which the Queen, amid national rejoicing, had been crowned in Westminster Abbey, and it would have made an admirable climax if Her Majesty had won the Derby with her high-mettled Hyperion colt Aureole. At the same time a victory for Sir Victor Sassoon's Pinza would have been almost equally popular. Pinza's rider, Sir Gordon Richards, had just been deservedly knighted for his services to racing, and so far success in the greatest of English races had eluded him. This was his 28th attempt and victory would indeed have been fitting for a man who had done so much to improve the image of racing and had justly earned the description of 'the punter's best friend'.

Pinza was bred by the great trainer, Fred Darling, who lasted just long enough to hear the result of the Derby and died 3 days later. A big, burly bay standing over 16 hands, Pinza was by the French-bred Chanteur II out of Pasqua, by the Italian-bred Donatello II. Imported into England by Mr William Hill, the well-known bookmaker, Chanteur II was a good, tough stayer; he won seven races in France and was second in the Grand Prix de Paris, while he won the Coronation Cup and two other races in England, besides being second in the Gold Cup twice. Pasqua never won herself and bred one other winner, the moderate Petros. In 1949 Mrs H E Morriss, whose husband owned the Banstead Manor Stud, had Pasqua covered by Chanteur II who was then standing at Banstead. As her first five foals had been disappointing, Pasqua was sent to the December Sales. Fred Darling, who was then convalescing in South Africa, saw her name in the catalogue, liked her pedigree and asked Mr J A Dewar to buy her for him, which he did for 2000 gns. When Darling came home and saw Pasqua he did not fancy her; she was again sent to the December Sales and an Argentinian breeder bought her for 525 gns. Pasca, by Manna, the dam of Pasqua, bred Pasch, winner of the Two Thousand Guineas and the Eclipse Stakes.

As a yearling Pinza was bought by Sir Victor Sassoon for 1500 gns and joined the Newmarket stable of Fred Darling's former head-lad Norman Bertie. The stable was to a large degree controlled by Jack Clayton who subsequently took out a licence to train himself. Pinza's first race at two was at Hurst Park in July. He was obviously still very backward but performed with encouraging promise for the future. That promise was amply fulfilled in the Tattersalls Sale Stakes at Doncaster in September which he won in a canter by six lengths. Later that month he started at 5–2 on in the one mile Royal Lodge Stakes at Ascot. There were only four runners, the pace was muddling and he managed to get beaten by the Aga Khan's filly Neemah. However, he ended the season in style by winning the seven furlongs Dewhurst Stakes at Newmarket by four lengths. In the Free Handicap he was given 9 st 2 which was 5 lb less than Nearula.

Pinza was always liable to play up at home and during the winter he got rid of his rider, fell on a gravel path and gashed his forearm. The injury was by no means serious and he soon appeared to recover. However, he then fell lame again and it was eventually discovered that a small piece of gravel had not been extracted. This little episode caused him to miss the Two Thousand Guineas. His first race at three was the mile and a quarter Newmarket

Stakes. He looked very much on the big side and there was little confidence behind him, but he won with singular ease by four lengths. His Derby price was immediately cut from 33–1 to 8–1.

In the Derby Pinza started joint favourite at 5–1 with Aureole's stable companion Premonition, Aureole being on offer at 9–1. Coming down the hill to Tattenham Corner, Pinza had the good fortune to find an entirely trouble-free passage on the rails, and he moved up second to Shikampur who entered the straight with a clear lead of several lengths. Two furlongs from home Pinza swept majestically into the lead and from that instant the issue was never in doubt. He won unchallenged by four lengths from Aureole who ran on gallantly enough but never really looked like getting on terms. The winner was accorded a tumultuous reception which was proof of the warm affection felt for his rider by every section of the racing world. Sir Victor Sassoon had spent a fortune on bloodstock in his lifetime, and up till this Derby had hardly enjoyed the rewards he deserved. It is typical of the way things are apt to go in racing that Pinza and Sir Victor's second Derby winner, Hard Ridden, cost less than 2000 gns the pair.

In the King George VI and Queen Elizabeth Stakes at Ascot Pinza confirmed the Derby form with Aureole whom he defeated decisively by three lengths with Worden II third. Unfortunately, Pinza broke down not long afterwards and never raced again. At his best he was unquestionably a very good horse indeed. However, though markedly superior to Aureole on the racecourse, he was far less successful as a sire. Aureole was twice champion, but Pinza was very disappointing, his best winner being the triple Classic winner Sun Chariot's son Pindari who was third in the St Leger and won over £18 000. Pinza also sired Pinturischio who showed high promise at three and was heavily supported in the Derby ante-post market, one bookmaker in particular incurring heavy liabilities. Not long before the Derby, Pinturischio was 'got at' in his stable and so severely injured that he never saw a racecourse again. (*Illustration: page 110*)

SEA BIRD II (1965)

The pedigree of Sea Bird II hardly suggested he was likely to become one of the best horses to race in Europe this century.

Bred by his owner M. Jean Ternynck, a French textile-manufacturer, he was a chestnut with a white blaze and two stockings behind by the American-bred Dan Cupid, a son of the famous Native Dancer. In appearance a typical sprinter, Dan Cupid won three times in France at two and coming

The four Derby winners owned by Sir Victor Sassoon: Pinza, Crepello, Hard Ridden, St Paddy. (TRH Neame)

to England in the autumn, was second to Masham in the Middle Park Stakes. The following season he was unplaced in the Two Thousand Guineas and the Derby and it was commonly supposed that he did not stay. He made nonsense of that theory, though, by running the race of his life in the mile and a half Prix du Jockey Club in which he was only just beaten by a really good horse in Herbager. That effort was the peak of Dan Cupid's career and he trained off afterwards.

The most remarkable feature of the bottom half of Sea Bird II's pedigree is that not one of his five immediate dams won a race of any sort under the rules of a Jockey Club in any country. Sea Bird II himself was the second foal of his dam Sicalade, by Sicambre. The nearest Sicalade came to success was to finish second in a race at Maisons-Laffitte.

Trained at Chantilly by Etienne Pollet, Sea Bird II ran three times as a two-year-old. After a comfortably gained success in the Prix de Blaison, he faced a much more severe task in the seven furlongs Criterium de Maisons-Laffitte. He won

that event decisively, too, among those he defeated being Carvin, subsequently sire of Pawneese, winner of the Oaks and the King George VI and Queen Elizabeth Diamond Stakes. His final race that season was in the one-mile Grand Criterium at Longchamp worth that year over £24 000 to the winner. Pollet also ran Madame Widener's Grey Dawn, a grey by Herbager. Grey Dawn was favourite, Sea Bird II second favourite. Despite a rather slow start and running a bit wide at the bend, Sea Bird II finished a creditable second to his stable-companion in a field of 13. A number of shrewd judges, who saw him at Longchamp that day, were confident he would vanquish Grey Dawn if ever the two met again. It was Sea Bird II's solitary defeat.

Sea Bird II wintered well and he won his first race, the ten furlongs Prix Greffulhe at Longchamp in April, in a canter. It was then clear that he was going to be a force to be reckoned with in any company. On 16 May he lined up for the mile and a quarter Prix Lupin at Longchamp worth over £27 000 to the winner. The field was a strong one and included

Sea Bird II, 1965, (Dan Cupid—Sicalade), one of the easiest Derby victors in living memory.
(Agence APRH, P Bertrand et fils)

Cambremont, who had won the French Two Thousand Guineas, and the hitherto unbeaten Diatome who had won the Prix Noailles and was to win the Washington International at Laurel Park. Sea Bird II won as he pleased by half a dozen lengths. Immediately afterwards Pollet announced that Sea Bird II would go for the Derby, and the bookmakers at once installed him as favourite for that event.

The weather and the going alike were perfect on Derby Day. Sea Bird II, a hot favourite at 7–4, was, of course, the centre of attraction for the paddock critics. Standing just over 16 hands, he looked extremely hard and trained to the minute. He was particularly admired for his fine bold outlook and his exceptionally powerful quarters. As he walked round it was noticeable that he 'dished' with his off-fore. In his earlier races Pollet had fitted him with gaiters, but these were dispensed with on this occasion. There had been persistent rumours that Sea Bird II was highly-strung and might get upset in the long-drawn-out Derby preliminaries, but in fact he remained gratifyingly calm.

There is really little that needs to be said about the race itself, as Sea Bird II won with such consummate ease. His jockey, Pat Glennon, always had him in a handy position and the favourite was sixth at Tattenham Corner. With a quarter of a mile to go, Sea Bird II was still on the bit and ideally poised to deliver his challenge. Just below the distance he moved up to join I Say, the leader, and such was his acceleration that in half a dozen strides the race was virtually over. He won by two lengths from Meadow Court with I Say a length and a half away third. If Glennon had not seen fit to ease him in the final 50 yd, the margin would have been very much greater. Experienced observers were adamant they had never seen a Derby won more easily.

Sea Bird II ran twice subsequently. On 4 July he was an easy winner of the Grand Prix de Saint-Cloud. His final appearance came in Europe's richest prize, the Prix de l'Arc de Triomphe, that year worth £85 727 to the winner. The field was a strong one and included Reliance, a half-brother by

Tantième to the 1963 Derby winner Relko and himself winner of the Prix du Jockey Club, the Grand Prix de Paris and the Prix Royal Oak; the Russian champion, Anilin; Tom Rolfe, winner of the Preakness Stakes and the American Derby; Meadow Court, winner of the Irish Sweeps Derby and the King George VI and Queen Elizabeth Stakes; and Oncidium, winner of the Coronation Cup.

With 2 furlongs to go the excitement was intense as it was seen that the issue clearly lay between Sea Bird II and Reliance. The duel, however, was not destined to be a protracted one. When Glennon asked Sea Bird II for his effort, the chestnut simply flew and the unfortunate Reliance, unquestionably a great racehorse, was made to look like a second-class handicapper. Sea Bird II won by six lengths and Reliance was five lengths in front of Diatome. For its sheer brilliance it was a performance that will never be forgotten by those who witnessed it.

It was improbable that the all-powerful dollar would permit Sea Bird II, winner of £225 000, to remain in Europe, and he was promptly leased by Mr John Galbreath, who had previously leased the mighty Ribot, to stand at his Derby Dan Stud in Kentucky. Ribot never returned to Europe; Sea Bird II eventually did but only shortly before his death in 1973. He had not been an unqualified success as a sire, but he got Gyr who was runner-up to Nijinsky in the Derby, and that great filly Allez France whose victories included the French One Thousand Guineas, the French Oaks, the Prix Vermeille, the Prix d'Harcourt, the Prix Ganay (twice), the Prix d'Ispahan, the Prix Dollar and the Prix de l'Arc de Triomphe.

NIJINSKY (1970)

A feature of modern English racing has been the many glittering successes of horses bred in North America and trained in Ireland by Vincent O'Brien. Four horses in this category—Sir Ivor, Nijinsky, Roberto and The Minstrel—have won the Derby and by common consent the best of them was Nijinsky, the first horse to win the Triple Crown since Bahram in 1935.

Nijinsky was bred in Canada by Mr Edward P. Taylor who has done so much to increase the standard and prestige of the Canadian thorough-bred. In 1953 Taylor imported the English mare Lady Angela, by Hyperion, in foal to Nearco. The foal Lady Angela was carrying was Nearctic, a fast, courageous horse that was in training for four seasons and won 21 of his 47 races in Canada and the United States. In his first season at stud, Nearctic, a plainish horse notably long in the back,

was mated with Natalma, a far from handsome filly that had cow hocks and was very straight in front. She had racing ability, though, but met with an accident in her preparation for the Kentucky Oaks and was taken out of training. The union of Nearctic and Natalma resulted in Northern Dancer. In 1964 he was the best three-year-old, at any rate up to a mile and a quarter, in the North American Continent, winning the Kentucky Derby and the Preakness Stakes as well as the most important race in Canada, the Queen's Plate.

Northern Dancer was a compact, elegant little horse of beautiful quality that stood only 15 hands 2 in. In his second season at stud he covered Flaming Page, by Bull Page, likewise a winner of the Queen's Plate and second in the Coaching Club American Oaks. Flaming Page was a tall, rangy mare that needed careful handling on account of her fiery temper. The produce of this mating, Nijinsky, inherited the bold, intelligent head and the strong, sound limbs of his sire; from his dam he derived his length of body and leg and his highly-strung temperament.

On Vincent O'Brien's advice Mr Charles Engelhard, known as 'the Platinum King' and one of the richest men in the world, purchased Nijinsky as a yearling for $84 000 at the Woodbine Sales in Toronto. Trained by O'Brien, Nijinsky tended to be excitable and impatient and required great patience and restraint from O'Brien and his staff. Though a big horse that stood 16 hands 3 in when fully grown, Nijinsky came to hand reasonably early and on 12 July 1969 he won the six furlongs Erne Maiden Stakes at the Curragh. He followed that up by winning three of Ireland's most prestigious two-year-old events, the Railway, Anglesey and Beresford Stakes, all run at the Curragh. In the Beresford Stakes he was given quite a tough battle by Decies, winner of the Irish Two Thousand Guineas the following year. In his Irish races Nijinsky was ridden by the capable Liam Ward. When he came to Newmarket in October to contest the seven furlongs Dewhurst Stakes, he was partnered by Lester Piggott. The opposition in the Dewhurst Stakes was not of a formidable character, but it was impossible not to be impressed by the manner of Nijinsky's victory, and he was placed top of the two-year-old Free Handicap.

The following year Nijinsky won the Gladness Stakes as a preliminary to the Two Thousand Guineas, which he won convincingly despite sweating up profusely during the parade in front of the stands. In the Derby in which, as in the Guineas, he was ridden by Piggott, he had to face two strongly fancied competitors from France in Gyr, a Sea Bird II colt whose high promise had delayed the retirement of Etienne Pollet by a year; and Stintino, winner of the Prix Lupin. Gyr, a tall, lanky colt whom some unkind paddock critics thought bore a certain resemblance to a camel, came down the hill like a polo-pony and was in front approaching the distance. At that point Piggott gave Nijinsky a couple of sharpish reminders, and Nijinsky responded in the way that only a really good horse can, accelerating smoothly to win by two and a half lengths from Gyr, who subsequently won the Grand Prix de Saint-Cloud, with Stintino third. Nijinsky's Derby time of 2 min 34.68 s was the fastest since Mahmoud established the record of 2 min 33.8 s on hard, bare ground in 1936.

Ridden by Ward, Nijinsky won the Irish Sweeps Derby in a canter from Meadowville. With Piggott up in the King George VI and Queen Elizabeth Stakes at Ascot, he outclassed a field that included the 1969 Derby winner Blakeney; Crepellana, winner of the French Oaks; Caliban, winner of the Coronation Cup; Karabas, winner of the Washington International; and Hogarth, winner of the Italian Derby. Not long afterwards it was announced that he had been syndicated for $5 544 000 (£2 266 666 at the existing rate) to stand at Mr 'Bull' Hancock's Claiborne Farm in Kentucky where Mr Engelhard kept his mares.

Unfortunately, during the late summer Nijinsky contracted ringworm. It was a severe attack and he temporarily lost almost all the hair on one flank. He was able to run in the St Leger and won without apparent difficulty but the effort, following his indisposition, probably took more out of him than was realised at the time.

It came as a fearful shock, at least to the Anglo-Irish racing world, when in the Prix de l'Arc de Triomphe Nijinsky was beaten by Sassafras, winner of the French Derby. Some people were inclined to blame Piggott for leaving Nijinsky with too much to do, but a study of the film showed clearly that Nijinsky was well placed on the final bend and that, when he delivered his challenge, he was only three lengths behind the winner. About 150 yards from the finish he drew level with Sassafras, but at that point he faltered and veered to the left as Piggott wielded the whip with his right hand. Whatever the cause of the defeat, it was not Piggott's riding.

Probably by October Nijinsky, being a high-mettled colt, had had enough racing that season; he had certainly done a lot of travelling and had furthermore suffered from a debilitating infection. It looked an obvious case of taking the pitcher to the well too often when he ran in the Champion Stakes at Newmarket only 13 days after the Arc. He was in a highly nervous state before the race and the huge crowd that had come to admire him saw him vanquished by the five-year-old Lorenzaccio who frankly was not in the same class. It is kinder and fairer to remember Nijinsky on the day he won the big race at Ascot. On that occasion he was unquestionably a champion. (*Illustration: page 114*)

MILL REEF (1971)

The first American victory in the Derby was that of Mr Pierre Lorillard's Iroquois in 1881. There was not another one till Lester Piggot rode Mr R S Clark's Never Say Die to victory in 1954. In recent years, though, the North American thoroughbred has played a role of ever-increasing significance in European racing, and horses bred the other side of the Atlantic won the Derby in 1968, 1970, 1971, 1972, 1976 and 1977. Three of these winners—Sir Ivor, Nijinsky and Mill Reef—were horses of the very highest class; and though Mill Reef did not emulate Nijinsky by winning the Triple Crown, there are many experienced judges who declare him to have been the best of the three.

Mill Reef was bred and owned by Mr Paul Mellon, one of the most distinguished figures on the American Turf. While an undergraduate at Cambridge he acquired a taste for fox-hunting and English racing. Originally he had jumpers with the Hon Aubrey Hastings at Wroughton, and when Hastings died suddenly he continued to patronise the Wroughton stable which was then run by Ivor Anthony. Anthony was succeeded by Aubrey Hasting's son Peter Hastings-Bass who transferred the stable to Kingsclere and concentrated on flat racing in place of jumping. Mr Mellon remained a patron of the stable and continued to be one after Hastings-Bass had died all too young and Kingsclere came under the control of Ian Balding who was 30 years of age when Mill Reef arrived from America.

Mill Reef is a beautifully proportioned bay, full of quality and very difficult to fault, with a kindly and equable temperament. He is by Nasrullah's son Never Bend, a record stake-earner as champion two-year-old in America, but too headstrong to be equally successful in the Classics at three. He was, however, placed in the Kentucky Derby and the Preakness Stakes. Many who knew him well found it difficult to visualise a son of his winning the Derby. Milan Mill, Mill Reef's dam, never won. By Princequillo out of Virginia Water, by Count Fleet, she is a half-sister to Berkeley Springs, winner of the Cheveley Park Stakes and runner-up in both the One Thousand Guineas and the Oaks. Red Ray, dam of Virginia Water, was by Hyperion out of Infra Red and was bought as a two-year-old for 12 000 gns at the sale of Lord Portal's horses. Red Ray, who never ran and produced only two living foals, was a granddaughter of the famous Black Ray.

Nijinsky, 1970, by L. Sandys Lumsdaine. (The Jockey Club, Newmarket)

Mill Reef came to hand nice and early and enjoyed a thoroughly successful two-year-old season. His one defeat came in the Prix Robert Papin at Maisons-Laffitte when he was narrowly, and perhaps a shade unluckily, beaten by the English-trained My Swallow, a colt of exceptional maturity and speed who went on to win the Prix Morny, the Prix de la Salamandre and the Grand Criterium. Mill Reef won the five furlongs Salisbury Stakes at Salisbury by five lengths; the six furlongs Coventry Stakes at Royal Ascot by eight lengths; the six furlongs Gimcrack Stakes at York in very heavy going by ten lengths; the six furlongs Imperial Stakes at Kempton Park by one length, his least impressive performance; and the seven furlongs Dewhurst Stakes at Newmarket by four lengths. In the Free Handicap My Swallow received 9 st 7, Mill Reef 9 st 6, and Brigadier Gerard, unbeaten winner of the Middle Park Stakes, 9 st 5. It was a long time

since there had been three such good two-year-olds in one season.

At three Mill Reef began on the right note by winning the seven furlongs Greenham Stakes at Newbury. Most people regarded the Two Thousand Guineas as virtually a match between him and My Swallow. There were only six runners and those two went off in front at a great pace. With 2 furlongs to go, both were under pressure but could find no more. Then along came Brigadier Gerard full of running to pass them as if they had been a couple of telegraph-poles. He won by three lengths from Mill Reef who beat My Swallow by three parts of a length for second place. It was a common view that Mill Reef and My Swallow had cut each others throats. At that stage of the season it was not widely realised how good a horse Brigadier Gerard was.

Brigadier Gerard did not run in the Derby. There seemed every possibility that Mill Reef would win that race, provided he stayed the distance. A lot of people doubted his ability to last out 1½ miles, but in fact Balding had satisfied himself on that point. Favourite at 100–30 and ridden as usual by Geoff Lewis, Mill Reef was always in a handy position. With 2 furlongs to go he accelerated in the smoothest possible fashion and ran on without the slightest sign of weakening to win by two lengths from Linden Tree with Irish Ball third. It was a thoroughly convincing performance that owed nothing to good fortune.

After the Derby Mill Reef went from strength to strength. In the Eclipse Stakes he outclassed the much-fancied French colt Caro who, in 1977, sired the winners of both the French Derby and the French Oaks. At Ascot Mill Reef won the King George VI and Queen Elizabeth Stakes by six lengths. His greatest triumph, though, came in October when he won the Prix de l'Arc de Triomphe by three lengths. He was voted 'Horse of the Year',

somewhat to the chagrin of certain of Brigadier Gerard's admirers who pointed out that the Brigadier had beaten Mill Reef fairly and squarely the only time they met.

Both Mill Reef and Brigadier Gerard remained in training at four, and it was hoped that a return match would take place in the Eclipse Stakes. Mill Reef did not look at his best in the paddock before the mile and a quarter Prix Ganay at Longchamp, but he put up a brilliant performance to win by ten lengths. His next race was the Coronation Cup at Epsom. Again he did not please the paddock critics, and on this occasion he took years off the life of one big backer in beating Homeric by a neck. Homeric was not held in particularly high esteem at this point in his career, but in fact he was a really good horse and would in all probability have won the Arc in the autumn (he finished third) if he had not broken down a furlong out.

Soon after Epsom, Mill Reef went down with the

Mr Paul Mellon's Mill Reef (Never Bend—Milan Mill) who won twelve races, including the 1971 Derby, before being retired to the National Stud at Newmarket. There he has sired 1978 Derby winner Shirley Heights and 1978 French Derby winner Acamas. (Fiona Vigors)

virus which afflicted so many stables that summer. He had to miss the Eclipse Stakes won by Brigadier Gerard, while a minor mishap stopped him from running in the Benson and Hedges Gold Cup at York, the race in which Brigadier Gerard sustained his solitary defeat. It was hoped that Mill Reef would win the Arc again, but at the end of August disaster struck and he broke a leg exercising at Kingsclere. Thanks to highly skilled veterinary treatment and the patience, courage and co-operation of the patient, this great horse was happily saved for the stud. He had won over £172 000 in England, over £135 000 in France.

Mr Mellon generously permitted Mill Reef to remain in this country. He was syndicated for £2 000 000, a British record, and stands at the National Stud. To begin with, he did not set the Thames on fire as a stallion, but in 1978 his reputation was established when his sons Shirley Heights and Acamas won the Derby and the French Derby respectively. He finished the 1978 season as champion sire.

SECTION 4

Derby Stakes winners

		OWNER	TRAINER	JOCKEY	SP
1780	Diomed	Sir C Bunbury	—	S Arnull	6–4
1781	Young Eclipse	Major D O'Kelly	—	C Hindley	10–1
1782	Assassin	Lord Egremont	—	S Arnull	5–1
1783	Saltram	Mr Parker		C Hindley	5–2
1784	Sergeant	Colonel D O'Kelly	—	J Arnull	3–1
1785	Aimwell	Lord Clermont	—	C Hindley	7–1
1786	Noble	Mr Panton	—	J White	30–1
1787	Sir Peter Teazle	Lord Derby	—	S Arnull	2–1
1788	Sir Thomas	Prince of Wales	—	W South	5–6
1789	Skyscraper	Duke of Bedford	—	S Chifney, sen.	4–7
1790	Rhadamanthus	Lord Grosvenor	—	J Arnull	5–4
1791	Eager	Duke of Bedford	—	M Stephenson	5–2
1792	John Bull	Lord Grosvenor	—	F Buckle	4–6
1793	Waxy	Sir F Poole	R Robson	W Clift	12–1
1794	Daedalus	Lord Grosvenor	—	F Buckle	6–1
1795	Spread Eagle	Sir F Standish	—	A Wheatley	5–2
1796	Didelot	Sir F Standish	—	J Arnull	—
1797	(Colt by Fidget)	Duke of Bedford	—	J Singleton	10–1
1798	Sir Harry	J Cookson	—	S Arnull	7–4
1799	Archduke	Sir F Standish	—	J Arnull	12–1
1800	Champion	Mr Wilson	—	W Clift	7–4
1801	Eleanor	Sir C Bunbury	—	J Saunders	5–4
1802	Tyrant	Duke of Grafton	R Robson	F Buckle	7–1
1803	Ditto	Sir H Williamson	—	W Clift	7–2
1804	Hannibal	Lord Egremont	—	W Arnull	3–1
1805	Cardinal Beaufort	Lord Egremont	—	D Fitzpatrick	20–1
1806	Paris	Lord Foley	—	J Shepherd	5–1
1807	Election	Lord Egremont	—	J Arnull	3–1
1808	Pan	Sir H Williamson	—	F Collinson	25–1
1809	Pope	Duke of Grafton	R Robson	T Goodison	20–1

Year	Horse	Owner	Trainer	Jockey	Odds
1810	Whalebone	Duke of Grafton	R Robson	W Clift	2–1
1811	Phantom	Sir J Shelley	—	F Buckle	5–1
1812	Octavius	R Ladbroke	—	W Arnull	7–1
1813	Smolensko	Sir C Bunbury	—	T Goodison	Evens
1814	Blücher	Lord Stawell	—	W Arnull	5–2
1815	Whisker	Duke of Grafton	R Robson	T Goodison	8–1
1816	Prince Leopold	W Lake	—	W Wheatley	20–1
1817	Azor	J Payne	R Robson	J Robinson	50–1
1818	Sam	T Thornhill	W Chifney	S Chifney, jun.	7–2
1819	Tiresias	Duke of Portland	—	W Clift	5–2
1820	Sailor	T Thornhill	W Chifney	S Chifney, jun.	7–2
1821	Gustavus	J Hunter	—	S Day	2–1
1822	Moses	Duke of York	—	T Goodison	6–1
1823	Emilius	J Udney	R Robson	F Buckle	11–8
1824	Cedric	Sir J Shelley	—	J Robinson	9–2
1825	Middleton	Lord Jersey	Edwards	J Robinson	7–4
1826	Lapdog	Lord Egremont	Bird	G Dockeray	50–1
1827	Mameluke	Lord Jersey	Edwards	J Robinson	9–1
1828	Cadland	Duke of Rutland	—	J Robinson	4–1
1829	Frederick	W Gratwicke	J Forth	J Forth	40–1
1830	Priam	W Chifney	W Chifney	S Day	4–1
1831	Spaniel	Lord Lowther	—	W Wheatley	50–1
1832	St Giles	R Ridsdale	—	W Scott	3–1
1833	Dangerous	I Sadler	—	J Chapple	30–1
1834	Plenipotentiary	S Batson	—	P Conolly	9–4
1835	Mündig	J Bowes	J Scott	W Scott	6–1
1836	Bay Middleton	Lord Jersey	—	J Robinson	7–4
1837	Phosphorus	Lord Berners	—	G Edwards	40–1
1838	Amato	Sir G Heathcote	R Sherwood	J Chapple	30–1
1839	Bloomsbury	W Ridsdale	W Ridsdale	S Templeman	25–1
1840	Little Wonder	D Robertson	W Forth	W Macdonald	50–1
1841	Coronation	A Rawlinson	—	P Conolly	5–2
1842	Attila	Colonel Anson	J Scott	W Scott	5–1
1843	Cotherstone	J Bowes	J Scott	W Scott	13–8
1844	Orlando	Colonel Peel	Cooper	E Flatman	20–1
1845	The Merry Monarch	W Gratwicke	J Forth	F Bell	15–1
1846	Pyrrhus the First	J Gully	J Day	S Day	8–1
1847	Cossack	T Pedley	J Day	S Templeman	5–1
1848	Surplice	Lord Clifden	J Kent	S Templeman	Evens
1849	The Flying Dutchman	Lord Eglinton	Fobert	C Marlow	2–1
1850	Voltigeur	Lord Zetland	R Hill	J Marson	16–1
1851	Teddington	Sir J Hawley	A Taylor	J Marson	3–1
1852	Daniel O'Rourke	J Bowes	J Scott	F Butler	25–1
1853	West Australian	J Bowes	J Scott	F Butler	6–4
1854	Andover	J Gully	J Day	A Day	7–2
1855	Wild Dayrell	F Popham	Rickaby	R Sherwood	Evens
1856	Ellington	Admiral Harcourt	T Dawson	T Aldcroft	20–1
1857	Blink Bonny	W I'Anson	W I'Anson	J Charlton	20–1
1858	Beadsman	Sir J Hawley	G Manning	J Wells	10–1
1859	Musjid	Sir J Hawley	G Manning	J Wells	9–4
1860	Thormanby	J Merry	M Dawson	H Custance	4–1
1861	Kettledrum	Colonel Towneley	Oates	R Bullock	16–1
1862	Caractacus	C Snewing	Zachary	J Parsons	40–1
1863	Macaroni	R Naylor	Godding	T Challoner	10–1
1864	Blair Athol	W I'Anson	W I'Anson	J Snowden	14–1
1865	Gladiateur	Count de Lagrange	T Jennings	H Grimshaw	5–2
1866	Lord Lyon	R Sutton	J Dover	H Custance	5–6
1867	Hermit	H Chaplin	Bloss	J Daley	1000–15
1868	Blue Gown	Sir J Hawley	J Porter	J Wells	7–2
1869	Pretender	J Johnstone	T Dawson	J Osborne	11–8
1870	Kingcraft	Lord Falmouth	M Dawson	T French	20–1
1871	Favonius	Baron de Rothschild	J Hayhoe	T French	9–1
1872	Cremorne	H Savile	W Gilbert	C Maidment	3–1
1873	Doncaster	J Merry	P Peck	F Webb	45–1
1874	George Frederick	W Cartwright	T Leader	H Custance	9–1
1875	Galopin	Prince Batthyany	J Dawson	J Morris	2–1
1876	Kisber	A Baltazzi	J Hayhoe	C Maidment	4–1
1877	Silvio	Lord Falmouth	M Dawson	F Archer	100–9
1878	Sefton	W Crawfurd	A Taylor	H Constable	100–12
1879	Sir Bevys	'Mr Acton'	J Hayhoe	G Fordham	20–1
1880	Bend Or	Duke of Westminster	R Peck	F Archer	2–1
1881	Iroquois	P Lorillard	J Pincus	F Archer	11–2
1882	Shotover	Duke of Westminster	J Porter	T Cannon	11–2
1883	St Blaise	Sir F Johnstone	J Porter	C Wood	11–2
1884	St Gatien	J Hammond	R Sherwood	C Wood	100–8
1884	Harvester	Sir J Willoughby	J Jewitt	S Loates	100–7

Year	Horse	Owner	Trainer	Jockey	Odds
1885	Melton	Lord Hastings	M Dawson	F Archer	75–40
1886	Ormonde	Duke of Westminster	J Porter	F Archer	4–9
1887	Merry Hampton	'Mr Abington'	M Gurry	J Watts	100–9
1888	Ayrshire	Duke of Portland	G Dawson	F Barrett	5–6
1889	Donovan	Duke of Portland	G Dawson	T Loates	8–11
1890	Sainfoin	Sir J Miller	J Porter	J Watts	100–15
1891	Common	Sir F Johnstone	J Porter	G Barrett	10–11
1892	Sir Hugo	Lord Bradford	T Wadlow	F Allsopp	40–1
1893	Isinglass	H McCalmont	J Jewitt	T Loates	4–9
1894	Ladas	Lord Rosebery	M Dawson	J Watts	2–9
1895	Sir Visto	Lord Rosebery	M Dawson	S Loates	9–1
1896	Persimmon	Prince of Wales	R Marsh	J Watts	5–1
1897	Galtee More	J Gubbins	S Darling	C Wood	1–4
1898	Jeddah	J Larnach	R Marsh	O Madden	100–1
1899	Flying Fox	Duke of Westminster	J Porter	M Cannon	2–5
1900	Diamond Jubilee	The Prince of Wales	R Marsh	H Jones	6–4
1901	Volodyovski	W C Whitney	J Huggins	L Reiff	5–2
1902	Ard Patrick	J Gubbins	S Darling	J H Martin	100–14
1903	Rock Sand	Sir J Miller	G Blackwell	D Maher	4–6
1904	St Amant	L de Rothschild	A Hayhoe	K Cannon	5–1
1905	Cicero	Lord Rosebery	P P Peck	D Maher	4–11
1906	Spearmint	Major E Loder	P Gilpin	D Maher	6–1
1907	Orby	R Croker	J Allen	J Reiff	100–9
1908	Signorinetta	E Ginistrelli	E Ginistrelli	W Bullock	100–1
1909	Minoru	King Edward VII	R Marsh	H Jones	7–2
1910	Lemberg	'Mr Fairie'	A Taylor	B Dillon	7–4
1911	Sunstar	J B Joel	C Morton	G Stern	13–8
1912	Tagalie	W Raphael	D Waugh	J Reiff	100–8
1913	Aboyeur	A P Cunliffe	T Lewis	E Piper	100–1

Craganour came in first, beating Aboyeur by a head, but was disqualified.

Year	Horse	Owner	Trainer	Jockey	Odds
1914	Durbar II	H Duryea	T Murphy	M MacGee	20–1
1915†	Pommern	S Joel	C Peck	S Donoghue	11–10
1916†	Fifinella	E Hulton	R Dawson	J Childs	11–2
1917†	Gay Crusader	A W Cox	A Taylor	S Donoghue	7–4
1918†	Gainsborough	Lady Douglas	A Taylor	J Childs	8–13
1919	Grand Parade	Lord Glanely	F Barling	F Templeman	33–1
1920	Spion Kop	Major G Loder	P Gilpin	F O'Neill	100–6
1921	Humorist	J B Joel	C Morton	S Donoghue	6–1
1922	Captain Cuttle	Lord Woolavington	F Darling	S Donoghue	10–1
1923	Papyrus	B Irish	B Jarvis	S Donoghue	100–15
1924	Sansovino	Lord Derby	Hon G Lambton	T Weston	9–2
1925	Manna	H E Morriss	F Darling	S Donoghue	9–1
1926	Coronach	Lord Woolavington	F Darling	J Childs	11–2
1927	Call Boy	F Curzon	J Watts	E C Elliott	4–1
1928	Felstead	Sir H Cunliffe-Owen	O Bell	H Wragg	33–1
1929	Trigo	W Barnett	R Dawson	J Marshall	33–1
1930	Blenheim	HH Aga Khan	R Dawson	H Wragg	18–1
1931	Cameronian	J A Dewar	F Darling	F Fox	7–2
1932	April the Fifth	T Walls	T Walls	F Lane	100–6
1933	Hyperion	Lord Derby	Hon G Lambton	T Weston	6–1
1934	Windsor Lad	HH Maharaja of Rajpipla	M Marsh	C Smirke	15–2
1935	Bahram	HH Aga Khan	F Butters	F Fox	5–4
1936	Mahmoud	HH Aga Khan	F Butters	C Smirke	100–8
1937	Mid-day Sun	Mrs G B Miller	F S Butters	M Beary	100–7
1938	Bois Roussel	P Beatty	F Darling	E C Elliott	20–1
1939	Blue Peter	Lord Rosebery	J L Jarvis	E Smith	7–2
1940*	Pont l'Eveque	F Darling	F Darling	S Wragg	10–1
1941*	Owen Tudor	Mrs MacDonald-Buchanan	F Darling	W Nevett	25–1
1942*	Watling Street	Lord Derby	W Earl	H Wragg	6–1
1943*	Straight Deal	Miss D Paget	W Nightingall	T Carey	100–6
1944*	Ocean Swell	Lord Rosebery	J L Jarvis	W Nevett	28–1
1945*	Dante	Sir E Ohlson	M Peacock	W Nevett	100–30
1946	Airborne	J E Ferguson	R Perryman	T Lowrey	50–1
1947	Pearl Diver	Baron G de Waldner	C Halsey	G Bridgland	40–1
1948	My Love	HH Aga Khan	R Carver	W Johnstone	100–9
1949	Nimbus	Mrs M Glenister	G Colling	E C Elliott	7–1
1950	Galcador	M Boussac	C Semblat	W Johnstone	100–9
1951	Arctic Prince	J McGrath	W Stephenson	C Spares	28–1
1952	Tulyar	HH Aga Khan	M Marsh	C Smirke	11–2
1953	Pinza	Sir V Sassoon	N Bertie	G Richards	5–1
1954	Never Say Die	R S Clark	J Lawson	L Piggott	33–1
1955	Phil Drake	Mme L Volterra	F Mathet	F Palmer	100–8
1956	Lavandin	P Wertheimer	A Head	W Johnstone	7–1
1957	Crepello	Sir V Sassoon	N Murless	L Piggott	6–4
1958	Hard Ridden	Sir V Sassoon	J Rogers	C Smirke	18–1
1959	Parthia	Sir H de Trafford	C Boyd-Rochfort	W H Carr	10–1

1960	**St Paddy**	Sir V Sassoon	N Murless	L Piggott	7–1
1961	**Psidium**	Mrs Arpad Plesch	H Wragg	R Poincelet	66–1
1962	**Larkspur**	R R Guest	M V O'Brien	N Sellwood	22–1
1963	**Relko**	M F Dupré	F Mathet	Y Saint-Martin	5–1
1964	**Santa Claus**	J Ismay	J Rogers	A Breasley	15–8
1965	**Sea Bird II**	J Ternynck	E Pollet	T P Glennon	7–4
1966	**Charlottown**	Lady Z Wernher	G Smyth	A Breasley	5–1
1967	**Royal Palace**	H J Joel	N Murless	G Moore	7–4
1968	**Sir Ivor**	R R Guest	M V O'Brien	L Piggott	4–5
1969	**Blakeney**	A Budgett	A Budgett	E Johnson	15–2
1970	**Nijinsky**	C W Engelhard	M V O'Brien	L Piggott	11–8
1971	**Mill Reef**	P Mellon	I Balding	G Lewis	100–30
1972	**Roberto**	J W Galbreath	M V O'Brien	L Piggott	3–1
1973	**Morston**	A Budgett	A Budgett	E Hide	25–1
1974	**Snow Knight**	Mrs N Phillips	P Nelson	B Taylor	50–1
1975	**Grundy**	Dr C Vittadini	P Walwyn	P Eddery	5–1
1976	**Empery**	N B Hunt	M Zilber	L Piggott	10–1
1977	**The Minstrel**	R Sangster	M V O'Brien	L Piggott	5–1
1978	**Shirley Heights**	Lord Halifax	J Dunlop	G Starkey	8–1

†Run at Newmarket from 1915 to 1918.
*Run at Newmarket from 1940 to 1945.

MISCELLANEOUS STATISTICS

Fastest winning times at Epsom:
2 min 33⅘ s—Mahmoud in 1936 (average speed 35·06 mph).
2 min 34 s—Hyperion in 1933.
2 min 34 s—Windsor Lad in 1934.
Richest prize: £111 825.50 for Nelson Bunker Hunt, owner of the 1976 winner Empery.
Record field: Most runners—34 in 1862. Fewest runners—4 in 1794.
Shortest priced winner: 2–9—Ladas in 1894.
Longest priced winner: 100–1—Jeddah in 1898, Signorinetta in 1908, and Aboyeur in 1913.
Smallest winner: 14 hands 3½ in—Little Wonder in 1840.
Largest winning margin: 8 lengths—Manna in 1925.
Winning fillies: Eleanor in 1801, Blink Bonny in 1857, Shotover in 1882, Signorinetta in 1908, Tagalie in 1912 and Fifinella in 1916.
Winning greys: Gustavus in 1821, Tagalie in 1912, Mahmoud in 1936, and Airborne in 1946.
Winning black horses: Smolensko in 1813, Grand Parade in 1919.
Dead heats: 1828 when Cadland beat The Colonel in the run-off. 1884 with Harvester and St Gatien—the stakes were divided.
Disqualifications: Running Rein in 1844, and Craganour in 1913.
Starting stalls: First used 1967.

OWNERS

Most wins: 5—3rd Earl of Egremont in 1782, 1804, 1805, 1807, and 1826.
4½—HH Aga Khan III in 1930, 1935, 1936, 1952, and a half share in 1948.
4—John Bowes in 1835, 1843, 1852, and 1853.
4—Sir Joseph Hawley in 1851, 1858, 1859, and 1868.
4—1st Duke of Westminster in 1880, 1882, 1886, and 1899.
4—3rd Duke of Grafton in 1802, 1809, 1810, and 1815.
4—Sir Victor Sassoon 1953, 1957, 1958, and 1960.

TRAINERS

Most wins: 7—Robert Robson in 1793, 1802, 1809, 1810, 1815, 1817, and 1823.
7—John Porter in 1868, 1882, 1883, 1886, 1890, 1891, and 1899.
7—Fred Darling in 1922, 1925, 1926, 1931, 1938, 1940, and 1941.
6—Matthew Dawson in 1860, 1870, 1877, 1885, 1894, and 1895.
5—Vincent O'Brien in 1962, 1968, 1970, 1972, and 1977.

JOCKEYS

Most wins: 8—Lester Piggott in 1954, 1957, 1960, 1968, 1970, 1972, 1976, and 1977.
6—Jem Robinson in 1817, 1824, 1825, 1827, 1828, and 1836.
6—Steve Donoghue in 1915, 1917, 1921, 1922, 1923, and 1925.
5—John Arnull in 1784, 1790, 1796, 1799, and 1807.
5—Frank Buckle in 1792, 1794, 1802, 1811, and 1823.
5—William Clift in 1793, 1800, 1803, 1810, and 1819.
5—Fred Archer in 1877, 1880, 1881, 1885, and 1886.
Youngest winning jockey: 16—J. Parsons in 1862.
Oldest winning jockey: 60—J. Forth in 1829.

Index

Illustration references in *italics*

OTHER GUINNESS SUPERLATIVES TITLES

Facts and Feats Series:

Air Facts and Feats, *3rd ed.*
John W R Taylor, Michael J H
Taylor and David Mondey

Rail Facts and Feats, *2nd ed.*
John Marshall

Tank Facts and Feats, *2nd ed.*
Kenneth Macksey

Car Facts and Feats, *2nd ed.*
edited by Anthony Harding

Yachting Facts and Feats
Peter Johnson

Business World
Henry Button and Andrew
Lampert

Music Facts and Feats
Robert and Celia Dearling with
Brian Rust

Art Facts and Feats
John FitzMaurice Mills

Soccer Facts and Feats
Jack Rollin

Animal Facts and Feats
Gerald L. Wood FZS

Plant Facts and Feats
William G. Duncalf

**Structures – Bridges, Towers,
Tunnels, Dams . . .**
John H. Stephens

Weather Facts and Feats
Ingrid Holford

Astronomy Facts and Feats
Patrick Moore

Guide Series:

**Guide to French Country
Cooking**
Christian Roland Délu

Guide to Freshwater Angling
Brian Harris and Paul Boyer

Guide to Saltwater Angling
Brian Harris

Guide to Field Sports
Wilson Stephens

Guide to Mountain Animals
R P Bille

Guide to Underwater Life
C. Petron and J B Lozet

Guide to Motorcycling, *2nd ed.*
Christian Lacombe

Guide to Bicycling
J. Durry and J B Wadley

**Guide to Waterways of Western
Europe**
Hugh McKnight

Guide to Water Skiing
David Nations OBE and
Kevin Desmond

Guide to Steeplechasing
Richard Pitman and
Gerry Cranham

Other Titles:

The Guinness Book of Answers,
2nd ed.
edited by Norris D. McWhirter

The Guinness Book of Records
edited by Norris D. McWhirter

The Guinness Book of 1952
Kenneth Macksey

The Guinness Book of 1953
Kenneth Macksey

The Guinness Book of 1954
Kenneth Macksey

Kings, Rulers and Statesmen
Clive Carpenter

History of Land Warfare
Kenneth Macksey

History of Sea Warfare
Lt-Cmdr Gervis Frere-Cook
and Kenneth Macksey

History of Air Warfare
David Brown, Christopher
Shores and Kenneth Macksey

English Pottery and Porcelain
Geoffrey Wills

Antique Firearms
Frederick Wilkinson

**The Guinness Guide to Feminine
Achievements**
Joan and Kenneth Macksey

The Guinness Book of Names
Leslie Dunkling

100 Years of Wimbledon
Lance Tingay

**The Guinness Book of British
Hit Singles,** *2nd ed.*
edited by Tim and Jo Rice, Paul
Gambaccini and Mike Read

**The Guinness Book of World
Autographs**
Ray Rawlins

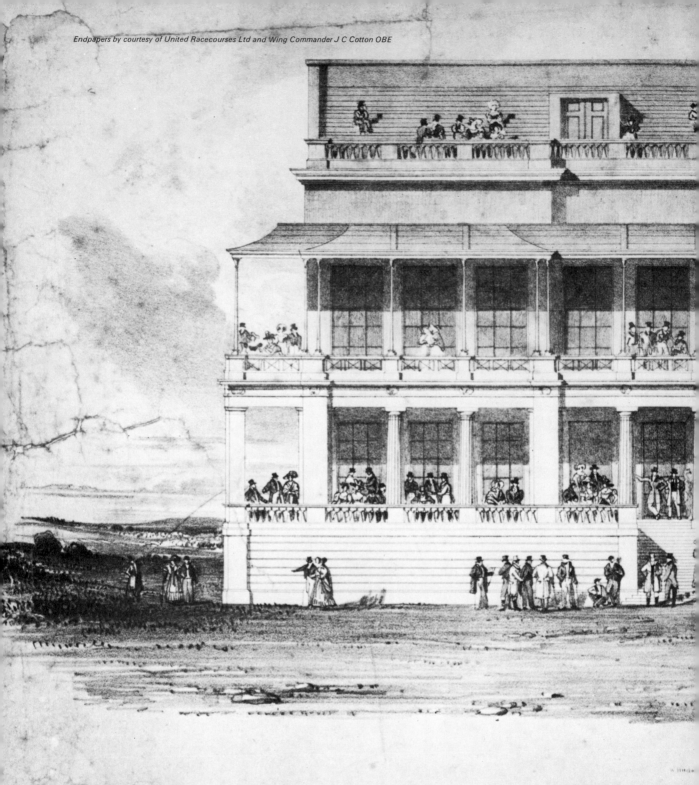

THE NEW

ERECTING O

...iation has been formed for the purpose of building this Magnificent Stand, capable of accommo...